BUTCHERING DEER

THE COMPLETE MANUAL OF FIELD DRESSING, SKINNING, AGING, AND BUTCHERING DEER AT HOME

OUTDOORSMAN'S EDGE®
GUIDES

BUTCHERING DEER

THE COMPLETE MANUAL OF FIELD DRESSING, SKINNING, AGING, AND BUTCHERING DEER AT HOME

John Weiss

CRE**A**TIVE
OUTDOORS™

Trade paperback edition frist published in 2004 by

CRE**A**TIVE
OUTDOORS™

An imprint of Creative Homeowner®, Upper Saddle River, N.J.
Creative Homeowner® is a registered trademark of Federal Marketing
Corporation.

Front Cover Photo: Dan Thornberg
Back Cover Photos: Bookspan Studios
Author Photo: John Weiss
Cover Design: Design Source Creative Services
Inside images by John Weiss unless otherwise indicated.

Printed in the United States of America
Current printing (last digit) 10 9 8 7 6 5 4 3 2
Library of Congress card number: 2004103773
ISBN: 1-58011-220-X

CREATIVE HOMEOWNER®
24 Park Way
Upper Saddle River, NJ 07458

Table of Contents

Foreword

Man's Connection with Venison
from Past to Present

On a windy, biting cold day more than 32,000 years ago a small band of big-game hunters found themselves huddled near a driftwood fire on the Kamchatka Peninsula in northern Siberia.

Modern scholars will later refer to that period as The Last Ice Age. Moreover, to put that time frame into perspective, it should be noted that the bow and arrow will not be invented for another 22,000 years. Pilgrims will not wade ashore in Massachusetts for another 310 centuries.

The Siberian hunters are nomads, they are hungry, and due to events about to unravel, their destination is unknown even to them. The only life they know is that of following the region's massive herds of caribou, bison, and mammoth as they migrate northward during summer, then south again at the approach of winter. During the summers the band of hunters, accompanied by women and children, supplement their spartan diets with flower buds and bird eggs, and during the winters they grub for roots. But year-round, the meat of the big-game animals they kill is their primary staple, while animal hides serve their clothing and shelter needs.

On this particular day, the strategy of these early nomads is, as usual, fairly well defined. Upon spotting a herd of caribou, the men quickly don antlered hoods to make themselves less conspicuous and then split into two groups, one of which slowly approaches and begins to mingle with the animals as they placidly graze upon lichens and moss. Then, when given a hand signal, the second group, this one consisting of the women and children, diverts the attention of the caribou with loud shouts, allowing the men to rush unsuspecting, nearby animals and plunge long spears into their bellies and ribs.

Three of the beasts stagger and then fall from their wounds and the hunters quickly reduce the meat to large chunks with knives consisting of flint blades hafted to short stick handles. The women and children meanwhile use the sharp edges of clam shells to scrape flesh from the hides before rubbing them with a mixture of tallow and brains to prevent the skins from hardening.

Later, after retreating from the raw weather to their skin tents, they use strips of sinew and needles made from antler slivers to begin fashioning boots, knee-length parkas, and replacement panels for their worn shelters.

Since fuelwood is scarce on the tundra, much of the meat is eaten raw. Small quantities that are to be saved for the journey ahead are sun-dried.

The Siberian hunters have no idea that this fateful year they will not be completing their return trip south, for they are about to become actors in a drama of discovery. The wandering herds of big-game animals continue onward still farther north, entering a narrow isthmus of land later to be named Beringia, and the hunters follow. It is a dry-land bridge, newly created when glacial activity reached its peak and locked up in ice millions of cubic miles of precipitation that would normally have gone into the oceans. The absence of this water lowered the level of the Bering Sea more than three hundred feet, enough to turn the shallows of the Bering Strait into a dry corridor connecting the continents of Asia and North America.

As the migrating herds of caribou and mammoth pass across the narrow fifty-six-mile land bridge, their numbers are squeezed together and the hunters have little trouble sandwiching small groups of animals between men armed with spears. Fuel, in the form of driftwood washed ashore, is now plentiful, and entire animal haunches are roasted over crackling flames in a community fire pit.

Now, let's fast-forward 5,000 years. Man is still a primitive creature and is not destined to invent the wheel for yet another 22,000 years. Christ will not be born for another 27,000 years. And Italian, Spanish, and Portuguese sailors will not make various claims of discovering the New World for another 230 centuries, yet already the northern hemisphere of that continent is being populated by the first true Americans. They are descendants of the nomadic big-game hunters from Asia, and upon completing their journey across the Beringia land bridge they find terrain they've never encountered before. To the north are polar seas and vast sheets of ice more than a mile thick. To the west is sub-arctic tundra, and to the south a combination of rain forests, fjords, and expansive mountain ranges.

Over the course of the next 10,000 years, many of these tribes continue to infiltrate what is now interior Alaska. In time they call themselves either "Eskimos" or "Aleuts," but by any name their foremost means of subsistence remains big-game hunting. Although a small percentage of these hunters choose to remain in their newly settled homeland, larger numbers of their brethren continue their nomadic lifestyles and continue south. Eventually their sons and daughters will skirt the unglaciated foothills of what is now called the Brooks Range. From there, grandchildren of those sons and daughters will press onward down the valley of the MacKenzie River and onto the broad plains east of the Rockies. Future generations will take a different route, following the later-named Yukon Valley southward through British Columbia and into what are now Washington and Oregon states. Their common bond is that none of them know the steadily retreating glaciers behind them are now melting and clogging northern river systems that drain into the ocean. Nor do they know that the Bering Sea is slowly rising again and thereby swallowing the dry-land bridge Beringia, sealing their fate and forevermore preventing them from returning to their ancestral homelands in Asia.

Future descendants of the earliest hunters continue to live by the daily rule of "hunt or starve," and by the year 12,000 B.C. they'll have gradually drifted still farther south into what will later be California and the desert Southwest. In canyon cliffs, some hunters are beginning to build multistory housing complexes which their Navajo descendants will later call pueblos. Other hunters, still restless from their ingrained nomadic heritage, push eastward onto the plains, where they live in huts fabricated from bark and grass. Still others penetrate what will later be Idaho, Montana, Wyoming, and the Dakotas. From there, their great-grandchildren will push into the lush Missouri, Mississippi, and Ohio River valley regions and then on to the Atlantic Coast.

By now, glaciers have continued to retreat to the extent that the landscape of the Americas, once two-thirds covered with water, is becoming drier with every passing century. Creatures previously acclimated to expansive miles of bogs and marshlands seem unable to adapt to their changing environments, and over the next several thousand years hundreds of species succumb to nature's timetable and become extinct. In their places other species, previously fewer in number, begin to thrive as the changing habitat now becomes conducive to their particular needs.

Wherever marginal wetlands still remain, there is Cervacles, an ancestor of our present-day moose, along with beaver and otter. At times, hundreds of thousands of plover and other waterfowl species form living blankets on these waters, and at the slightest disturbance stain the entire sky black for endless periods. On the prairies vast herds of bison, elk, and antelope graze upon sedges and broomgrass, and mature forestlands that spring up become inhabited by bears, foxes, turkeys, and coyotes.

Man is still a hunter, but in his travels he has begun to relish the comfort of the warmer southern climes; with the arrival of each summer he finds himself more and more reluctant to follow the caribou herds back to the polar regions of the far North. In making this decision, his acquired taste for venison is not satisfied except for those infrequent times when he succeeds in driving Cervacles up to its withers in deep swamp muck, where the hapless creature may then be dispatched with spears.

All along there have long been other types of deer on the hoof–mule deer, blacktails, and whitetails, all of which developed sometime in the Pleisto cene Epoch more than 700,000 years ago–but with the majority of the landscape now either deeply wooded or open prairie, the habitat is not attuned to their browsing preference and this keeps their numbers to a minimum. Also, the hunters quickly learn that these deer are so swift, alert, and elusive that attempting to sneak close enough to fell one of the cunning animals with a spear is largely a futile endeavor.

For the time being, man therefore contents himself with the pursuit of bison. They're available in enormous numbers, the meat is good, the hides are warm, and the animals have poor vision, making them relatively easy prey. Hunting is still largely a cooperative effort, and entire herds of bison are stampeded over the edges of cliffs and into deep gullies where their falling, crushing weight spells their demise.

We're still in what modern archaeologists call Prehistory, an early period of time for which there are no written records. What we know–and there's often heated debate among scientists as to exactly what happened, when, and where–has been pieced together through carbon-dating examination of man's rudimentary hunting tools, kill sites, and the camps he established.

Now fast-forward 10,000 years. Man still depends heavily upon the killing of animals for food, but instead of tirelessly pursuing herds of big game, he is spending much of the year living in semi-permanent communities. Anthropologists will later refer to these people as Paleo-Indians, although individual tribes such as the Llano, Folsom, Clovis, and Plano cultures become as widespread geographically as they are diverse in customs. Following, in thousands of years, will be the Archaic-Indians, and these in turn will be followed by the predominant Adena and Hopewell cultures of the Woodland-Indian period. Not until sometime around A.D. 1500 will these hunters and gatherers be labeled "American Indians" or "Native Americans."

It's the Paleo-Indian hunters that are first to reacquaint themselves with venison. The reunion comes about through the birth of the atlatl, an ingenious device that allows an individual to throw his spears far greater distances and with greater speed than was previously possible with strictly hand-thrown weaponry.

By description, an atlatl is a two-foot-long wooden handle with a bone hook on one. The butt of a six-foot-long spear is then hollowed out to accept the atlatl's hook. By grasping the atlatl's handle in the palm, and supporting the spear above with two raised fingers, the Indian achieves an extension of his arm—gaining a distinct mechanical advantage—that allows him to take a much wider arc in swinging his arm and thereby propel the spear three times faster than otherwise, and with surprising accuracy.

The invention of this unique device comes at an opportune time because herds of bison, while still in evidence, are steadily diminishing in number. The Indians subsequently shift their interests to elk, antelope, and deer, which now, through the aid of the atlatl, can be taken with a higher degree of regularity. Worth noting is that it's the whitetail and mule deer that now begin receiving the focus of attention, for the hunters quickly learn that elk and antelope prefer open prairie ground where they are difficult to approach, and if unduly molested they will run for miles. The deer, on the other hand, cling to the edges of thick cover and can be ambushed from close range.

It's also interesting to note that the so-called "arrowheads" one commonly sees today in museums and sometimes even finds during the course of outdoor adventures aren't really arrowheads at all; the bow and arrow, while in full use in Europe and throughout the Middle East, is not destined to arrive on the North American scene for yet another 9,000 years. Thus, so-called arrowheads, which are much too large to have been used to tip arrows, should more accurately be referred to as spearheads, as they were initially used to tip hand-thrown weapons and then later those hurled through the assistance of an atlatl. True arrowheads, not to be used by American Indians until much later, were tiny, seldom more than one-half inch in length, as anything heavier and larger would have greatly impeded an arrow's flight.

Now let's turn our time machine on again to bring us to A.D. 1290, when various forms of the word "veneison" begin appearing in common use among English sailors. Derived from the Latin venatio, meaning "the fruits of the hunt," the first known incidence of its use is found in a ship's log dated May 10. On that date the Captain of the Seahawk, bound for Madrid, penned a notation in the provision's ledger, "to Huy nomen with heom into heore schip i-novz bred and wyn, venesun of heort and hynd, and of wild swyn, reminding himself to take onboard for the jou ney enough bread and wine, venison of male and female deer, and wild boar."

For the next one hundred years there is no uniform spelling of the word, nor specific definition, and its pronunciation varies: uneysun, venysoun, wenysoun, venson, or vinzun. Sometimes the reference is to deer, but other times it is used to describe boar, hare, rabbit, or the red meat of almost any other wild animal.

It's sometime around 1400 that "venison" is gradually being refined to mean solely the meat of deer. The first of these explicit references comes from the rural English countryside where Squire Lowe Degre, after a successful hunt, describes the eating of Storkes and snytes and venyson freshe of bucke and do. Then, in 1598, an author known only as "Manwood" writes in the English journal Lawes Forest that Amongst the common sort of people, nothing is accompted (equal to) the venison fleshe of Red and Fallow Deere.

During this same time frame, in the Americas, various Indian cultures from coast to coast have almost entirely abandoned the use of the atlatl for throwing their spears. They've learned from foreign traders that much smaller shafts only two feet in length can be propelled with astonishing speed and accuracy by using a flexible length of wood drawn tense with sinew stretched between the opposite ends. The bow and arrow allows hunters to begin enjoying venison more frequently than ever before.

It's time to fast-forward again, now to the year 1620. It was one hundred twenty-eight years ago that Christopher Columbus landed his ships Santa Maria, Pinta, and Nina on the shores of the Bahamas. But 1620 is a hallmark year when William Bradford and his Pilgrim followers establish Plymouth Colony on the shore of Cape Cod Bay in Massachusetts. They find the countryside profusely wooded and inhabited by "savages" and numerous wildlife species.

The Indians—Delawares, Penobscots, Iroquois—have long since become proficient with their bows and arrows, but deer are not plentiful in the climax forests east of the Appalachians, so the Indians often employ gang-hunting tactics for acquiring their venison. Sometimes they form long lines that advance through miles of wooded tracts, the "drivers" beating hollow gourds against tree trunks to make whitetails flee in the direction of other hunters waiting in ambush farther ahead. Another ploy is setting fire to the woodlands, and as the wind fans the blaze, the hunters wait along down-wind vantage points for alarmed deer to come racing by. Still other times deer are driven into lakes or wide rivers, where they are helpless and duly clubbed by Indians in canoes. Many of the deer are roasted whole over enormous fires to feed entire villages where all are clothed in durable, light-weight buckskin.

The Pilgrims quickly learn to savor the New World's venison, using a forerunner of the shotgun, called a blunderbuss, which has a flared muzzle that sprays a lethal charge of lead balls when an ounce of black powder is ignited by a spark.

While Indians are cooking their venison over open fires, and occasionally in clay jars filled with water, the colonists use heavy, black implements they call "cast iron," which they have brought with them from the Old World. There are high-sided frypans and bowl-shaped, three-legged pots with capacities ranging from only one quart to huge vessels holding twenty-five gallons. But the classic Dutch oven, fitted with a wire bail and a concave lid with a flange around the perimeter for holding coals, will not gain widespread fame for another one hundred fifty years, when pioneers begin heading west in Conestoga wagons.

As individual family units and small groups of settlers sever their umbilical ties with the New England colonies in order to explore the new frontier, the eastern whitetail population begins a slow and steady increase–a direct result of dramatic changes brought upon its habitat. For the first time ever, deciduous forests hear the ring of the axe and the clang of plowshares as log cabins are built and wooded tracts are cleared for agricultural purposes. Even the continued burning of woodlands throughout the Midwest as a hunting method by the Cheyenne, Shawnee, and Cherokee is beneficial to the whitetail, for the random, checkerboard elimination of high-canopy forests promotes a variety of regenerative vegetation and understory. As the food dramatically increases, so does the reproductive rate of the deer.

By now, the blunderbuss has been replaced by the Kentucky long rifle, and several decades later these flintlocks will yield to percussion-cap rifles. Men with names such as Boone, Bridger, and Crockett are gaining national acclaim for their hunting exploits and shooting prowess.

In 1816 Eliphalet Remington establishes the Remington Arms Company, and fifteen years after that smokeless powder is born. In 1867 the first rifle bearing the name "Winchester" appears on the market, and the Model 73 becomes one of the frontier's most popular arms. Venison continues to play an incredibly important role in the diets of pioneer families who rely upon stews as a means of stretching their precious meat.

In 1893 a thirty-year-old genius by the name of Henry Ford invents the gasoline engine, and within the next twenty-four years he will build and sell more than fifteen million automobiles. Sixty years after that man will make use of another type of vehicle, called Apollo, to visit the moon and, as irony would have it, the return flight brings the ship's orbit down and across the Kamchatka Peninsula and Bering Sea. In 1893, however, frontier families, trappers, traders, and cowboys are still struggling to tame the wild lands west of the Mississippi. Passage of the Homestead Act 30 years earlier has been encouraging them by the thousands to steer their wagons in search of cost-free farmlands.

For several decades buffalo herds have been declining at an alarming rate and this adds to the reliance frontier families place upon venison: East of the Continental Divide it's whitetail venison, but as westward-bound pioneers penetrate the foothills of the Rockies, mule deer, previously utilized only by Indians, become subjected to intense hunting pressure almost overnight. For forty years, gold-mining camps from Oregon to California have already been making a serious dent in the blacktail population, consuming thousands of tons of the venison every year.

Meanwhile, throughout the East, small settlement towns have long since been transformed into burgeoning cities and trade centers. America is entering an age of unprecedented development and industrialization, and its appetite for venison as a tasty and inexpensive meat source seems to have no bounds.

Numerous states, sensing the venison bubble about to burst, have been attempting correctional measures for many decades. In Virginia, a law has been on the books for a century that prohibits the killing of does. Pennsylvania, Connecticut, and New York have almost simultaneously adopted laws that regulate the seasons during which deer can be harvested. In most cases, seasons are closed from February through August to ensure maximum reproductivity of the animals. Yet although such laws are well-intentioned, they are largely unenforceable.

There is no way to know exactly how many deer the nation possessed before The Great Decline. However, trading company logbooks do exist and give us a vague idea of the enormity of the deer kill during the years 1830 to 1900.

One New York hunter living in the Adirondacks, Thomas Meacham, is known to have killed at least 2,500 deer over a span of twenty-nine years. For eleven consecutive years, an average of 80,000 deer were killed annually in Michigan. A Delaware hunter brought to a trading post eighteen deerskins per week for forty-seven consecutive weeks. Hundreds upon hundreds of barrels of venison and tall stacks of salted hides arrived almost daily in growing eastern cities by freighter canoe, river barge, wagon, and mule train.

To make matters even more tenuous, lavish hotels, restaurants, and boarding houses in New York City, Philadelphia, St. Louis, and other major cities demanded only prime cuts of venison to please their wealthy clientele. Adding to the whitetail's trouble in the East and Midwest, and the mule deer and blacktail's predicament in the West, meat buyers in France, Great Britain, and other foreign countries began taking their toll, thereby aggravating an already serious situation. Indeed, eating venison was no longer relegated to serving the subsistence lifestyles of America's poor rural, but had become a popular pastime in the richest palaces of the world.

Thousands of men found they could earn a better living as market hunters than by remaining in factories or behind horse-drawn plows. They became known as superior marksmen with shooting skills honed to perfection. It became a matter of personal pride to take twenty cartridges hunting and return with twenty deer and not a pound of the choicest "money meat" damaged.

It is now 1900, and the majority of the country's deer have been either exterminated or pushed into remote regions still not penetrated by mankind on a regular basis. In Pennsylvania, New York, and New Jersey, news that a hunter has succeeded in killing a deer makes front-page headlines, for most people have not even seen a deer in these states for many years and have switched their meat-eating reliance to domesticated livestock. States have just begun keeping records, and many of them are sadly reporting that for all practical purposes deer are extinct in their regions.

Yet amidst this ominous news there is a glimmer of hope, because this is the year the hunter-financed conservation movement is born. Market hunting is outlawed, and nearly all states begin implementing wildlife management programs spearheaded by competent biologists. Prominent naturalists begin coming to the forefront of national attention. Men such as Teddy Roosevelt, his Chief Forester Gifford Pinchot, George-Bird Grinnell, and John Audubon, and organizations such as the Sierra Club and the Boone and Crockett Club call loudly for the establishment of strict seasons and bag limits. Hunters begin buying licenses to fund the work of their state agencies and a new type of occupation—game warden—now employs hundreds. A new era is dawning in which man, for the first time in his history, no longer chooses—or is allowed—to hunt indiscriminately or as a means of subsistence. Deer hunting in particular has become a "sport," strictly governed by the laws of the states and the rules of fair chase.

With this startling turn in the hunting history of man, deer populations begin to increase slowly in select regions. In those few states where they even begin to flourish, it becomes feasible to live-trap a percentage of the animals and use them for restocking in states where the herds are so depleted that they are unable to increase their kind through natural succession alone.

It is now 1937. The federal government has just implemented the Pittman-Robertson Act (also known as the Federal Aid to Wildlife Restoration Act), partly in response to the requests of sportsmen. Hunters want to do more, and not just for deer and other game species but for all wildlife. They realize that many regions have become so depleted of wildlife that greater financial help is needed than that generated through the sale of hunting licenses alone. Another growing threat to wildlife is also becoming apparent, in the continuing growth of cities and urban areas.

Each year, tens of thousands of acres of prime habitat is bulldozed away for housing developments and industrial uses.

Through the Pittman-Robertson Act, dollars contributed by hunters purchase more than four million acres of wildlife habitat in the next forty-five years. An additional one billion dollars is raised through special excise taxes that hunters pay when purchasing firearms, ammunition, and archery equipment, with the money subsequently channeled into management programs that benefit game and non-game species alike. These efforts by hunters and their conservation agencies begin having a tremendous impact upon deer populations nationwide.

It is now 1983. From a low of 350,000 deer at the turn of the century, their numbers have spiraled upward to an astounding seventeen million, which is far more than when Indians and Pilgrims sought their venison. Pennsylvania, which was one of the states that only fifty years ago had to request transplanting stock from other regions due to its virtually nonexistent herd, now boasts a population of more than one million whitetails. Texas leads all other states with more than six million deer–twenty times as many as existed in all the states combined less than sevnty-five years ago!

As further testimony to the success of the conservation movement, many states are beginning to lengthen their seasons and also are allow-ing–even encouraging–hunters to take does.

It is now 2002 and in New Jersey and portions of New York it is possible almost any evening to see herds of dozens of whitetails grazing placidly in open meadows like so many beef steers.

An Ohio population survey reveals the Buckeye State now is home to half a million whitetails, despite an annual hunter harvest averaging 185,000 animals, and this surge in whitetail numbers is bringing with it many problems; in the most recent twelve-month period there have been nearly 25,000 reports of deer-related vehicle accidents on highways. In many regions east of the Mississippi, soaring deer populations are causing extensive crop damage and, especially near large metropolitan areas, they are invading suburban neighborhoods and decimating expensive ornamen-tal shrubs and trees.

In an attempt to remedy the situation, many states allow hunters who apply for special permits to take ten or more deer per season. In other states, Alabama being just one example, hunters may take one deer per day throughout a lengthy season that spans four months.

In the 30,000 years that have passed since early man first stepped into the New World, he clearly has experienced dramatic cultural and techno-logical changes. Instead of wearing clothes made from caribou hides and sleeping on the dirt floor of a grass hut, modern man wears a three-piece suit of synthetic fibers and lives and works in buildings of concrete, steel, and glass. Instead of a daily philosophy of "hunt or starve," he has become almost totally reliant upon the agricultural pursuits and livestock-raising efforts of others.

Yet despite these major transformations in his lifestyle, he's never lost his hunting instinct, for man is fundamentally a predatory animal and no predator's genetic urges can be entirely dulled by time. As social situations require, he may succeed in temporarily repressing such drives, yet somewhere below the surface of his personality they remain an integral part of his being.

How else to explain the fact that each year an estimated twenty-two million hunters representing a wide cross-section of our modern society venture afield to hunt deer which nationwide now exceed thirty million in number? How else to explain their willingness, in fact eagerness, to endure weather extremes, physical discomfort, and other hardships with no assurance their efforts will culminate in success?

On an individual level, any hunter's motivations for deer hunting can be examined from many perspectives. But despite the occasional bonus of impressive antlers, the quest for prime venison always has and always will be a primary motivator.

Not only is properly prepared venison delicious but nutritionists say It's higher in protein and lower in fat than most domesticated meats. For example, 100 grams of trimmed, prime-grade beef has 17.4 grams of protein and 25.1 grams of fat. In comparison, an equal quantity of venison has 21 grams of protein and only four grams of fat. In addition to being low in fat, venison is also low in cholesterol; according to the Department of Agriculture (USDA), only buffalo and ostrich are lower.

Of special importance to health-oriented families, venison is unlike domesticated meats in another important regard: It is not impregnated with artificial coloring dyes, flavor enhancers, preservatives, and numerous other chemical additives that we are just beginning to discover may have long-term damaging effects upon ourselves and our children.

Clearly, man's quest for venison has been as ageless as time itself; no other food has been as inextricably woven throughout the fabric of his existence in both the New and Old Worlds.

Yet this phenomenon presents an intriguing question. Modern hunters have evolved from knapping their own flint spearheads to using high-tech firearms and hunting bows, so why take the effort to learn how to butcher your own deer? After all, deer processing facilities abound and most of them do a credible job; all that's necessary is to check a local newspaper's classified ad section or ask at the nearest general store in the area you're hunting.

Yet as easy as it is take this path, many hunters harbor mixed feelings about surrendering their animal to a deer processor.

Perhaps heading the list, many individuals feel there's something lacking in the satisfaction department when they conclude their hunt by bringing home to their family neatly wrapped packages of meat that are labeled, ready for the freezer, and don't appear entirely unlike those available at the supermarket.

They'd rather bring the entire animal home for view, and then custom-cut their venison to their own preferences and in meal portions best suited to their needs. Equally important, they'd much rather do the work themselves because it represents a further extension of their involvement with and commitment to their favorite outdoor pastime.

Unfortunately, many hunters lack the basic meat-cutting knowledge and self-confidence to attempt to reduce a one hundred-pound-plus animal carcass to succulent table fare.

This book will eliminate that apprehension by walking you through the various, easy steps with down-home logic that will make you wonder what you ever worried about. In little time, butchering your own deer will be a reward in itself, one that is every bit as fulfilling as taking the deer in the first place, and then serving any of the time-tested recipes also found within these pages.

–John Weiss

The Selective Deer Hunter

There is certainly no shortage of animals these days. Even trophy bucks abound. In fact, this season an estimated nine hundred of those deer will find their way into the Boone & Crockett or Pope & Young record books. Hunters will take millions of deer nationwide. With such a large number of deer available to the country's hunters, why shoot an animal that no one except perhaps the family dog will eat? You wouldn't go to the grocery store and put on a blindfold before making a large meat purchase, and then expect your family to suffer through months of tough, flavorless beef riddled with sinew and gristle. Why take that approach when entering the deer woods?

This year hundreds of deer will make the record books, while millions of others are destined for home freezers. That's something our ancestors could only have dreamed about.

Of course, as we saw in the Introduction, early man didn't have the luxury of being selective in his hunting. When you're hungry and must rely upon primitive equipment such as a spear to avoid starvation, you can't be fussy about what you kill. You take what comes along, and you're grateful for it.

Today's hunter lives in a different world. Undoubtedly, he owns a freezer that can preserve his game in excellent condition for many months—a distinct advantage over his predecessors. Moreover, early man hunted long and hard most every day of the year, and missed countless shots before eventually collecting game. Yet today's hunter, equipped with state-of-the-art shooting equipment, enjoys a thousandfold greater success rate in terms of hours spent afield.

We no longer need to hunt in order to eat, and so we no longer need to be opportunists. Yet counterbalancing this to some extent, today's hunter is restricted by season dates and the number of deer he can take in a given year.

The bottom line is that sensibility will, or at least should, govern the attitude of any hunter. He'll want to be selective in making his choices, to ensure that the animals he does take offer the best possible eating. If it turns out that the deer a hunter levels his sights upon yields delicious, tender venison and also is a buck with impressive antlers, then that hunter has the best of both worlds.

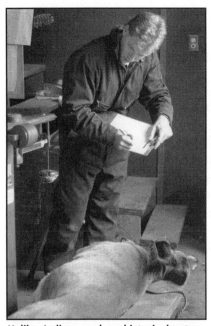

Unlike Indians and prehistoric hunters, today's deer hunter has the liberty of being able to look over many animals and evaluate their condition before deciding which to take.

Judging Tender Deer

Many myths surround the subject of what makes for a tender deer, but professionals in the food industry will tell you that the sex and age of the animal are not the most important considerations.

Components that go into the quality (tenderness and flavor) of virtually any game animal include: (1) the health of the animal at the time it was killed; (2) the diet of the animal throughout the year; (3) the amount of stress the animal was subjected to just prior to its demise; (4) the meat-handling techniques used from field to kitchen; and (5) the cooking method, since different cuts of meat require different cooking techniques. There is nothing a hunter can do to control the diets of deer, since they eat just about anything at one time or another. But over the years I've noticed that deer taken from rich agricultural regions, where they undoubtedly fed regularly upon corn, soybeans, alfalfa, oats, wheat, orchard fruits, and truck-garden vegetables, have been fatter and consistently more tender and flavorful than leaner animals killed far back in the hinterland where they subsisted mainly upon twigs, buds, leaves, weed species, wild grasses, and similar native foods.

One thing a hunter can do at the outset is evaluate the health of any animal in question before committing to squeezing the trigger or releasing the bowstring. Evaluating the health of a deer is not difficult, either; it can be accurately determined by merely examining its various body features.

Sometimes this is easier said than done, because few deer are enthusiastic about posing long minutes before a hunter wielding a .270-caliber rifle. And, of course, impulsive hunters who are more interested in shooting and getting their animal on the ground any way they can, and as quickly as possible, obviously have no way of evaluating the quality of their venison until after the fact. By then it's too late, and they must hope for the best because their hastily made decision is now irreversible.

But many times (I'm talking now about the careful, methodical hunter who plans his strategy and is selective about what he takes home), it is indeed possible to watch a deer for quite a while before deciding whether or not to try and collect it. By doing this, the hunter gains a valuable education for future hunts when he perhaps does not have so much time to look over a particular animal; then his accumulated experiences from the past allow him to merely glance at a deer and instantly know its worth. If and when a particular animal does not measure up to his expectations, he withdraws back into the shadows and continues to hunt, hoping to come across something better. Hunters derive immense pride and satisfaction from this type of hunting philosophy.

In evaluating a given deer, first check the color and condition of the animal's coat. This should take only a few seconds. Through the warm spring and summer months a deer's coat is made up of thin, solid, light-reddish-brown-colored hairs that allow body heat to escape and thereby render somewhat of a cooling effect. Later in the season, deer exchange their summer coats for dark-grayish-brown coats of thick, hollow hairs that efficiently

First check the animal's coat. It should glisten and be smooth and of uniform color.

trap body heat and provide them with warmth during the winter. These coats, in turn, will be shed sometime the following spring as air temperatures once again begin to climb.

If you spot a deer during the fall or winter hunting season and it is still sporting a reddish coat, something is wrong. That animal is not in good health and may not even make it through the coming winter. Unless you like using a linoleum knife to slice your steaks, you should wait for something better to come along.

Even a deer that has its characteristic gray-brown winter coat may be in poor health if that coat looks dull, lusterless, is ruffled in places, and overall has a scraggly looking appearance. This occurs when the coat hairs are no longer being supplied with naturally produced lanolin and other body oils normally secreted by the skin and hair follicles. In any species, this dysfunction is an indication of malnutrition or other ill health.

A deer in prime condition, on the other hand, has a coat that is smooth and thick, of uniform coloration or very gradual blending, with a rich, glossy sheen. There is no mistaking such deer. In fact, from the picture window of my southern Ohio farmhouse, I have a perfect view of our south meadow. And when the angle of the sun is just right, healthy deer seen from a distance actually appear to "shine" like bright lights, as the luster of their coats has a distinct reflective quality. There are often as many as a dozen whitetails on that meadow at the same time, attracted to a seven-acre food plot I've sowed into red clover, and I cannot recall ever taking a deer there that was not butterball fat and scrumptious table fare.

After learning to evaluate the condition of a deer's coat as a benchmark relating to the animal's health, next study the contours of the animal's musculature to determine whether the deer is "on the mend" or "on the skids."

Unlike livestock, which generally gain weight continually, wild animals frequently go through up and down periods during their lives. Winter, for example, is terribly hard on many species living in the North, and spring is generally considered a recovery period. In the deep South or arid West, however, midsummer may be difficult as well, due to heat waves, droughts, and insects and parasites that torment wildlife species; cool weather usually is the tonic that revitalizes them. In any of these situations, some animals may never recover from their setbacks, while others recuperate slowly, and still others bounce back almost immediately. Whatever the case, their present states of health are always reflected in their coats and the contours and shapes of their bodies.

Deer that are slowly and steadily gaining in weight are unanimously far more tender than those that haven't yet recovered from their setbacks or are slowly deteriorating in both physical health and body weight. A partial explanation for this is that anytime a living organism begins losing weight, fat stores are always the first to go. And it's the fat (called "marbling" by livestock growers), layered in muscles and woven through the fibers of the meat, that, during cooking, helps to break down that tissue structure and make it tender. Make note, we're not referring here to the "larding" an animal possesses–those thick layers of fat, usually across the rump and shoulders–but the thin, barely visible streaks of marbling fat between the meat fibers; deer, compared to livestock, are quite lean even when healthy, and losing what little marbling fat they do possess is disastrous to the final eating experience.

A good rule of thumb is to keep the word "round" firmly planted in your mind. Deer are active animals and are never larded or marbled to extremes, as livestock is. Nevertheless, vigorous, healthy, well-fed, tender-eating deer reveal distinctly padded, rotund curvatures no matter which particular area of the anatomy you're looking at.

Animals on the skids are equally easy to recognize. You'll be able to see clearly the animal's ribs through the skin, its vertebrae along the spine, sometimes even the vague outline of its pelvis. Likely, the animal's neck also will be thin, its muzzle may appear long and narrow rather than short and blocky, and its breastbone, where the lower neck joins the brisket, will protrude sharply outward.

Many times, a deer's antlers also reveal clues to his health, because food intake always goes first into body growth and maintenance. Only after these requirements have been satisfied are excess nutrients channeled into antler growth and development. Consequently, a buck carrying a rack that is thin,

Deer never become as fat as livestock, but do keep the word "round" in mind as a benchmark of the animal's physical health.
(photo by Michigan DNR)

spindly, and whitish may not have been feeding well. Look for thick, well-proportioned main beams and tines that are dark mahogany colored and perhaps white at the tips. You'll see these characteristics on healthy bucks of all ages, not just on trophies.

Similarly, antler growth and development is greatly influenced by trace mineral elements (primarily phosphorus and calcium) in the water deer drink. Some regions of the country are quite high in these nutrients while others are quite low. This explains why many specific regions continue, year after year, to produce large numbers of trophy bucks while other areas apparently equal in habitat and food value rarely produce impressive racks; deer in these latter regions may be just as healthy, overall, and just as tender and flavorful, but they simply do not have that little something extra in their diets that is conducive to large antler growth.

So don't let antlers alone fool you when ascertaining the health and eating qualities of any particular deer. Give the antlers a cursory inspection, to be sure, but let your final judgment be governed by the color and condition of the animal's coat and the appearance of its musculature. At lot of ballyhoo

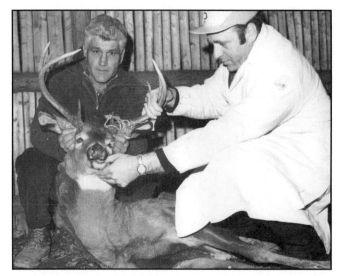

As a rule, young deer are more tender than old deer and does are more tender than bucks. This isn't always the case, however. Factors such as diet and how well certain animals survived the previous winter also play a role in the tenderness of their venison.

has also been circulated about killing only "dry" or "barren" does–those not presently lactating or beyond the age of bearing offspring–as their meat is supposedly more tender than that from a doe still capable of reproduction and which nursed newborn earlier in the year.

Truth be known, it's virtually impossible for anyone other than a biologist to determine if a doe is barren, and even he is incapable of such magic when the deer is on the hoof and in the wild. Deer biologists tell me they'd very much like to know how some hunters profess to shoot only barren does because it would be a boon to the scientific community. In actual hunting situations, things like this are just not verifiable. It's a moot point, anyway, because by the time late fall and early winter hunting seasons arrive, does that produced young in the spring have long since weaned their fawns and ceased lactating. Usually, the young ones, now completely independent and capable of surviving on their own, nevertheless continue to follow their mothers around, at least until they go into estrus during the rut and chase them away.

Another matter of debate has to do with the eating qualities of bucks in rut. Many deer hunters maintain that rutting bucks are virtually inedible, but the issue is not so cut and dried.

During the rut, males become so amorous they spend little time eating and resting. They're almost constantly on the move with pent-up sexual energy, the result of a sudden increase in the hormones released by their endocrine glands. In addition to territorial disputes with other bucks, a mature male may successfully breed with and impregnate dozens of does during the brief mating period. It should come as no surprise that this amount of continual courtship leaves him gaunt, worn, and exhausted.

One study has shown that a healthy buck weighing one hundred eight-five pounds just prior to the rutting period may be down to only one hundred forty pounds at the conclusion of the rut only two weeks later! It is this very phenomenon that accounts for a high degree of winter kill among bucks in the far northern states. Often, the deer simply do not have enough time to gain back their substantial weight loss before the onset of bitter cold weather, and this makes them not only subject to malnutrition and disease but also weak and vulnerable to predation. Such bucks are "on the skids" toward the tail end of the hunting season; because of their loss of body weight and tissue marbling, their musculature may be stringy and even have a somewhat blue-colored tinge.

Make no mistake, such bucks are still fully edible. They're generally just not as flavorful and tender as deer taken at other times. However, at butchering time, the hunter may wish to use the majority of this venison for burger, sausage, and stew meat, reserving only the backstrap and tenderloin steaks for the grill.

Yet bucks living in warmer climates, especially in agricultural regions where prime foods are in abundant supply, may not be so adversely affected because the delay or even total absence of cold weather allows them to begin a speedy recovery. Before the hunting season is only half over, they may already be on the mend, slowly but steadily recovering their lost body weight and replacing their marbling.

Generally, therefore, the best advice is this: the earlier in the season you kill your deer, the better.

If this is not feasible, I again emphasize, study the animal's general outline, its coat, its antlers, its musculature and other body features, looking for distinctive clues that tell in advance what type of meat you're likely to end up with on the butchering block and ultimately the table.

Does, by the way, are not subjected to the same degree of exhaustion and weight loss as bucks because their peaks of sexual activity are very brief. While a buck may be rut-crazed from daylight to dark for several weeks, does come into estrus (heat) for a single twenty-four-hour day. If they do not conceive during this period, they lose heat, return to a normal lifestyle, then recycle back into a second twenty-four-hour heat twenty-eight days later.

Fawns are a bit different. Actually, I dislike using the word "fawn" in conjunction with hunting activities because too many people, especially

This buck has a nice rack, but look closer. His coat is scraggly, his musculature is sinewy, and you can see his ribs. Take this deer and you'll get impressive antlers for the wall but mighty tough eating.

non-hunters, associate fawn with a just-born deer with a spotted coat and wobbly legs. There are no such fawns during the hunting season, only what biologists refer to as yearlings. Technically, they're not a year old but rather, at seven months of age, are in their first year of life, generally weigh sixty to seventy-five pounds and, from a survival standpoint, have reached the stage of independence from their mothers. These little buggers are often as crafty and elusive as adult deer. Likewise, their venison is usually quite tender.

Fawns born early in the season are weaned early. And since they've been on solid food for several months before hunting season, they've had time enough to acquire modest amounts of marbling in their muscle tissues. This musculature has not yet been subjected to extensive exercise and hardened-off, as with adult deer, which helps make them so tender.

Fawns born late, as a rule, prove just the opposite, simply because a doe that breeds during her second estrus period doesn't produce the same quality or amount of colostrum in her milk to give her newborn a headstart in the nutrition department the following spring. A hunter who desires to take a yearling should therefore pick one that appears unusually large in size, which is a sure giveaway that the deer is somewhat older, and then quickly shift his attention to the various body features described earlier.

I've discussed these points at length so that any hunter, once he has firmly seated in his mind what to look for, will be able to judge the quality of any given deer at a glance. I've seen wholesale buyers of beef cattle walk into a stock lot filled with steers and, in scant minutes, grade dozens of individual animals and their respective values. They know what to look for—which animals have prime carcasses, and which are below standard and best shipped to the pet food factory. Deer hunters can acquire similar skills.

Avoid Stressed Animals

Hunters can control to a certain extent the stress that any particular animal is subjected to just before being killed. And it stands to reason that deer that have been stressed minimally are destined to provide better eating than those that have been stressed excessively.

An explanation for this comes from food technicians, microbiologists, and wildlife specialists at Texas A & M University, where the subject has been studied intensively.

Stress can be defined as an unusually high metabolic rate resulting from significantly increased bodily functions. In other words, the organism's operating level, from both a mental and physical standpoint, has been strained far beyond its norm. In deer, this commonly occurs when the animal is chased long distances by predators such as dogs, pushed hard by hunters participating in drives, or is crippled or superficially wounded and is attempting to escape.

In these circumstances, adrenaline begins rapidly flooding the blood stream. Simultaneously, oxygen deprivation in the musculature allows the build-up of lactic acid and other waste residues that the animal's metabolic structure can no longer purge. If the deer in question is not injured and is able to escape and rest, the adrenaline flow eventually subsides, blood oxygen gradually increases and cleanses the animal's circulatory system of lactic acid and other wastes, and the animal shortly returns to a nonstress state of being.

However, if the animal is killed during the peak of its stress response, adrenaline and various acid wastes, instead of eventually dissipating, remain in the musculature. This is what's primarily responsible for what some not too fondly refer to as a strong or "gamey" flavor.

At the opposite extreme, a deer taken under nonstress conditions typically proves to offer tender, sweet, succulent meat. Normal heart rate, endocrine gland secretion, blood flow, kidney and liver functions, and overall body chemistry are such that the meat is not subjected to excessive acid contamination. This is precisely the reason why ranchers, before butchering beef or hogs, place them in tightly confined feedlots and corrals where the animals are not permitted to move around much. True, the flavor of venison is nearly always more "intense" than that of beef, but that can be attributed to nothing more than the sharply different diets of the animals.

One time, in western Kentucky, I was sitting in a blind watching the intersection of two deer trails. Far in the distance I could hear the shouts, hollers, and periodic volleys of shots resulting from numerous hunters staging a massive deer drive. About twenty minutes later, a nice six-point buck, which apparently had eluded the hunters, came loping by. It was easy to see that the deer had been running hard for a long distance. He was panting heavily, his head was rising and falling from exertion, and his tongue was hanging from his mouth as he tried to catch his breath. Although his antlers were not of taxidermy caliber, the buck's body was in splendid condition, and under any other circumstances I would not have hesitated to fill my tag right then and there. But I wanted a winter's supply of tasty steaks and roasts, not seventy-five pounds of dog food, so I let him go. Lesson learned.

Animals that are stressed, especially bucks that have just concluded the rut and lost substantial body weight, won't be as tender as you'd like until after they've gone through a recovery period to eliminate acid wastes from their bodies and rebuild their fat stores.

This is not meant to be a blanket condemnation of deer drives, because when they are executed properly the animals are not overly stressed. By properly, I mean using a small group of skilled, well-organized hunters who move through the woodlands without a great deal of commotion in an attempt to slowly nudge deer a relatively short distance to partners stationed ahead. In these cases, the deer seldom line out like jackrabbits heading for the next county. Instead, they generally slink and sneak along, trying to circle and dodge the drivers and standers, and they frequently provide easy shots. It's the huge, raucous gang hunts covering miles of terrain with spooked animals running hither and yon that typically result in stressed deer, superficially wounded deer, and venison that is not fit to eat.

2

Practical Tips on Shooting Your Deer

I t's been said that the best place to shoot a 1,200-pound moose is as close as possible to a flatbed truck where ten friends are waiting to help you load the beast. In some instances a one hundred fifty-pound deer might be an equally formidable challenge, which reminds me of a predicament I almost faced in West Virginia's New River Gorge.

My partner, Tom Harden, and I were peering down into a canyon bottom, watching a big whitetail feeding on honeysuckle growing on the chasm's rocky walls. The deer was one of the biggest either of us had ever seen. It must have walked five miles to get into that particular spot, and the shooting distance was an easy one hundred yards. Trouble was, that one hundred yards was straight down into a jungle of Volkswagen-sized boulders, scrub willows, and thornbrush. Nevertheless, I was about to squeeze the trigger when Tom brought me to my senses.

"If you kill that deer, how are we going to get him outta there?" he whispered. "Just getting down into that hellhole to field dress him will take rock-climbing expertise neither of us possess, and we can't afford to rent a helicopter with a skyhook."

When tempted to take a deer, always make a quick evaluation of the terrain to determine the ease with which the animal can be dragged, carried, or removed by vehicle. In some cases, hellacious real estate can prevent a hunter from recovering his deer.
(photo by Fiduccia Enterprises)

Lessons learned: always size up the terrain you plan to hunt in terms of safely getting in and out, and never shoot an animal in such a hellacious place that retrieving it borders on the impossible.

Shooting Ethics

This is just one example of the responsibilities we should all adopt afield. I'm not a preacher, and this is not the proper forum for preaching. It's about the many aspects involved in transforming a deer on the hoof into eventful dining fare. But simply selecting a particular recipe is not enough to achieve this end result. Long before the carcass ever reaches the butcher block, many other elements come into play that have their own telling influences. So we must carefully weave all of these threads into a tapestry that includes not just kitchen work but how and where the animal is shot, what the hunter does immediately after his game is on the ground, and so on.

Shooting behavior likewise plays a role in not only the quality of venison a hunter receives for his effort but also the quantity, and that reminds me of another anecdote.

Friend Jerry Burrows, a professional meatcutter who moonlights during the deer season by processing animals for hunters, tells me the most frustrating part of his work is having hunters accuse him of stealing their venison.

"If a field-dressed deer weighs one hundred forty pounds at a check station, many hunters seem to assume that's about how much edible meat they'll have for their freezer," Jerry explains. "Obviously this is not correct. You can't eat the hide, skeletal bones, lower legs and hooves, and other scraps, and that material may represent fifty percent of the animal. Then there's the damaged meat I often have to throw away that a hunter's misplaced shots have ruined."

One time, a hunter became so angry with the small amount of wrapped venison packages the processor had waiting for him that Jerry took him to a back workroom, where the remains of the hunter's deer carcass were still on a cutting table.

"Only you know how many times you shot at this deer," Jerry told the man, "but as you can see, the carcass you brought to me is so riddled with bullet holes it looks like Swiss cheese. I'm sorry I couldn't do more with it."

To be sure, the majority of deer hunters are respectable sportsmen who would never purposely misplace their shots and thereby turn prime roasts into dog food. But since this does happen, there are several inescapable conclusions. Most of us should probably spend more time practicing with our chosen shooting equipment and studying the anatomy of the game we're hunting. Further, we should all be far more selective in picking acceptable shots.

A good deal of personal honesty is part of this picture, for the stark truth is that some hunters are far more proficient with firearms and archery equipment than others, and some have stacked up many more years of in-field deer-hunting experience. As a result, two hunters who are evaluating the same shooting circumstances may come to entirely different conclusions as to whether a given shot can be attempted with a high level of confidence, whether the shot should be delayed until the animal's position changes, or whether the shot should be passed up altogether.

Regardless of any individual hunter's shooting skills, there are some shots that never should be attempted. One is when numerous deer are running together in tight formation and all that is visible through the sights are blurred glimpses of antlers partly obscured by flashes of doeskin.

One type of shot that should be passed is when several deer are intermingling and the animal you wish to take has most of its vital region obscured.

Another is the extremely long shot, far beyond the equipment's capability or at a distance the hunter has never before practiced at the target range. Still another is when a deer is only partly visible behind a screen of cover through which there are no clear shooting holes, and there's the likelihood of only superficially wounding the animal.

Knowing when, exactly, to take a shot is another paramount consideration that depends chiefly upon the existing circumstances, for, like fingerprints,

This shot angle is one frequently seen by bowhunters who hunt from high tree stands, but it's not recommended; there's too much chance the spine or the curvature of the rib cage will cause the arrow to glance away and miss the vitals.

no two encounters with deer are ever precisely alike. If I could set the stage and actually dictate perfect conditions for you, here's what I'd write into the script:

The deer would be close, well within the shooting range you've repeatedly practiced, yet completely unaware of your presence; it would be broadside to your line of aim, or quartering slightly away; it would be standing still or moving very slowly while either feeding or looking in some other direction; and, there would be little or no intervening cover.

This shot angle is perfect. But it's easy to see that the animal is stressed and breathing heavily from being pushed a long distance by drivers. Most hunters will shoot in this situation, but they should know in advance that the venison will not be prime.

Admittedly, such ideal conditions seldom occur on a regular basis. But the point to be made is that if you know what constitutes perfect shooting conditions, and diligently strive to set them up, you are then better able to make discriminatory judgment calls when less-than-ideal conditions prevail. This is the hallmark that separates the skilled, veteran hunter from the beginner. Instead of impulsively blasting away, the experienced hunter uses at least half of the fleeting moments awarded him to use his brain before his trigger finger.

The subject of shooting at running deer is likewise an inflammatory one. I have no objection to this practice, provided there is a reasonable chance of the hunter scoring an accurate shot and not excessively ruining much of the venison. This means, ideally, that a shot that presents itself should be one he has repeatedly practiced with moving targets on the shooting range, the distance should not be beyond his capabilities, and there should not be a great deal of intervening cover.

Beyond this, keep in mind what we said in the previous chapter about running deer being animals often in a state of high stress and suffering from adrenaline and lactic-acid build-up in their musculature. So quickly, answer this question. Is the running deer you are anticipating shooting at an unalarmed buck loping along behind a hot doe? Or, is it an animal racing for its life, having just escaped from a huge drive party in the next county?

Aiming Points

More than a century ago, those market hunters who were the most successful at their trade, and the best paid, were the ones who learned to pick their shots. They knew that those specific shots that were the surest and deadliest were also the ones that left virtually all of the prime venison—the money meat—undamaged.

Deer not subjected to hunting pressure dawdle endlessly, so do not be impulsive and shoot too quickly. Be patient and the animal will eventually offer a perfect broadside shot. (photo by Florida Game & Fish)

Actually, deer of all species possess many vital regions that, when penetrated, will result in the animal's demise, either sooner or later. However, many of these vital regions are quite small, which makes hitting them a questionable matter. And many others, although larger, require penetrating prime meat to reach them. Others are within such close proximity to prime meat that they're risky as well; if the shot is just a bit off, the animal may indeed expire, but there may be a good deal of collateral damage.

Ballisticians frequently demonstrate this point by firing bullets through blocks of gelatin and using high-speed cameras to record the action. But you can demonstrate the same phenomenon to yourself by investing a few bucks in a watermelon and shooting at it on a target range. Prop the melon up, so your bullet will travel lengthwise from one end through the center and out the other. The length of a watermelon is about the same distance as the width of a deer's body when the animal is standing broadside, and the inside of the melon fairly well simulates the organs, tissues, and fluids in a deer's body. You'll quickly see, upon shooting, that the slug does not merely pass through

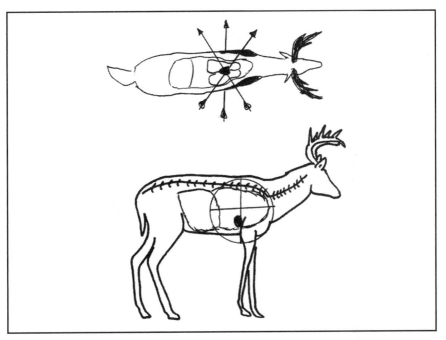

The most desirable aiming point is the heart-lung chest region immediately behind and slightly to the rear of the front shoulder. But keep in mind the shot will have to be slightly forward or behind the vitals to angle forward or to the rear if the animal is not standing perfectly broadside.

the melon's length and leave small entrance and exit holes. On the contrary, the instant the slug touches the melon's skin it begins expanding, and from there plows a large pathway the remaining distance. Furthermore, the speed of the slug generates massive shock waves that literally cause the melon to violently explode with large pieces flying in all directions.

A rifle slug passing through the body of a deer is not quite so dramatic, and even less so is that of a rifled shotgun slug, blackpowder bullet, or an archery broadhead. But all do indeed cause tissue damage—sometimes extensive—to those areas surrounding the projectile's path.

With this in mind, I've never understood the logic behind so many of the shots touted in hunting magazines and books previous to this one. I distinctly remember seeing one drawing where recommended aiming points were indicated on a deer running directly away. One such aiming point was the root of the tail, the claim being that a bullet hitting there would bring the deer down instantly by paralyzing the central nervous system, which is entirely true; what wasn't mentioned was the effect of the slug continuing to plow its way forward through the rump meat and then through the length of the loin steaks lying on either side of the backbone. The other recommended aiming point for a deer running directly away was squarely in the middle of one hind leg or the other, about halfway down from its attachment at the pelvis. A slug entering here, it was said, would sever the femoral artery and the deer would bleed to death in short order. True enough. But the author never mentioned that in taking such a shot you could kiss the entire hindquarter good-bye.

Almost as bad, I've seen recommendations about shooting for the spine when a deer is standing broadside. Again, the integrity of the central nervous system is so disrupted that the deer immediately hits the dirt like a sack of potatoes. But you can virtually forget about treating your family to venison chops.

Another shot I cannot recommend is the heart shot. A slug or arrow that hits the heart proves almost instantly fatal. If the deer does not drop on the spot, it will make a mad dash for fifty yards or so and then suddenly go down as if it fell into an abandoned well. But the heart lies much lower in the chest cavity than most hunters realize, and there's a good chance, if the slug or arrow is placed just a bit too far forward into the brisket region, or too far to the rear and therefore in the paunch, that the deer will escape and not die until it is far away. Even if the heart is squarely penetrated, the hunter may lose a good portion of both front legs, which are directly in front of that organ.

Head shots are also instantaneous in their results, but I rate them out of the question as well. The target is small and often moving just enough to greatly increase the risk of only wounding the deer, allowing it to escape, die, and go unrecovered.

Neck shots are "iffy." When the vertebrae of the neck are broken, the deer falls right in its tracks. But the neck is a relatively large target, and too many hunters have a tendency to aim right for the middle, not realizing that the actual vertebral column is situated in the upper one-third (toward the back of the neck). The esophagus and major arteries feeding the brain are located in the lower one-third, and a shot here will result in a wound from which the deer will eventually die, but often not then and there.

So neck shots are one of those dubious affairs. Many times the deer goes right down, but just as often it does not. Furthermore, those deer that are recovered, either on the spot or sometime later, typically have a good deal of damaged neck meat. It's not prime meat, to be certain, but it is a major cut for making burger, stew meat, or sausage.

If a deer is standing directly facing you, another neck-shot possibility is aiming for the white throat patch just below the chin. So hit, the deer is instantly dead; but again, it's a relatively small target, about the size of a grapefruit, and a shot that strays just a bit off-center may result in a deer that escapes and dies elsewhere.

Hunters should also be aware that head or neck shots predictably ruin the hide, skull, or antlers. This can be discouraging if the hunter wants to have his prize sent to a taxidermist, because the damage may be irreparable.

This brings us to the lung shot, which is the one I've always recommended to beginner and expert alike. It is instantly fatal, or nearly so, and therefore the animal does not experience a prolonged period of stress. Moreover, the lung is the largest vital target a deer possesses, which increases the chances of a successful shot.

The lung region is about the size of a basketball, and it lies between and slightly behind the two front shoulders. I always suggest aiming just a tad behind the front leg, as there is still plenty of lung material for the slug or arrow to penetrate and you avoid the otherwise regrettable loss of one or both front shoulders. If you study a deer's anatomy, you'll see this aiming point appears almost as a slight depression in the curvature of the ribs. It's the surest shot I know, and one that results only in a small loss of inconsequential rib meat. Since this aiming point also is quite far removed from contiguous musculature, there's rarely any collateral damage to any of the surrounding prime portions of venison.

The curious thing about this matter of where to aim is that a methodical, careful hunter who wants to facilitate a quick and merciful death of his deer, with no wasted meat whatsoever, simply does not need a number of shot-placement options. If he alone is in control of the shooting situation, and patiently waits until the animal is standing broadside or nearly so, he'll logically never have to consider anything but the lung shot.

It should be mentioned that there may be times when deer are not standing perfectly broadside but are just slightly quartering-away or quartering-forward. Shots such as these are fully justified if the angle is not too acute, but the hunter must remember to aim just a bit forward of the usual point of aim, or just a bit farther back, to ensure that the slug or arrow in turn angles forward (or backward) into the lung region.

Most hunters strive for a broadside shot that results in a double-lung hit, but quite often a quartering-away or quartering-forward shot angle results in only one lung perfectly penetrated while the off-side lung is only nicked. Nevertheless, this is acceptable because the shot angle, instead of squarely hitting the off-side lung, penetrates only the near-side lung but also penetrates the liver, which usually is just as fatal as a lung hit.

Tree-stand hunters face a slightly different shooting situation than that of ground-level hunters. Now, the slightly adjusted sight-picture for a slightly quartering-away, quartering-forward, or even a direct broadside shot must also be adjusted for a sometimes acute downward angle; the projectile must enter higher up in the back region, but below the backstraps, to squarely hit one or both lungs.

Moreover, bowhunters encounter yet another unique circumstance in that deer shot at commonly "jump the string." In other words, they dive into a crouched position, to coil their legs in order to bound away, and in so doing actually duck the flight of the arrow. To counter this, the accepted aiming

If there is a perfect shot, this is it! The animal is unalarmed, not moving, and just slightly quartering away.

point is now the heart. The lungs still are the desired contact point but if a hunter aims for the lungs, and the animal drops one-third of its body size when it crouches, the arrow will hit high in the spinal region or fly entirely over the back of the deer. Conversely, if the hunter aims for the heart, and the animal ducks, the arrow's path will carry it straight into the lung region.

So whether firearm hunter or archery hunter, never-ending year-round practice sessions on the target range are one of the prime ingredients that contribute to a successful outing.

At this point, you may be anxious for us to get on with the title subject of this book, which deals primarily with butchering, but I feel it has been necessary to first plow a bit of other ground. The end goal of course is to place succulent venison on the table. But even a professional butcher armed with every conceivable kitchen tool and recipe will fail to prepare tender, delicious venison steaks if the meat is ragged and bloodshot; in that case, the only beneficiary of the hunt is the family dog. The same is true even in the case of deer quickly and cleanly dispatched with a lung shot if the carcass and its attached venison is not cared for properly in the field, which is the subject of the next chapter.

Whenever possible, use a "rest" to stabilize the firearm and allow for pinpoint accuracy. If a log, boulder, or tree trunk is not immediately at hand, drop to a kneeling or sitting position.

3

Field Dressing Your Deer

Before you got lucky and filled your tag, things were much easier because whenever the going got tough you could pace yourself. But now, you're in a race against the clock. Lying before you is an animal that weighs one hundred eighty pounds. Sixty pounds of that consists of prime steaks and roasts, and there's another forty pounds of venison that will make excellent stew meat, sausage, and burger. And you know for sure you'll lose every ounce if you don't immediately prevent it from spoiling. You have to cool that meat as quickly as possible, then get it out of the woods and safely to home or camp. What you do in the next half-hour or so will largely determine the quality of the meat that reaches the butcher table and, later, your family's dinner table.

After your deer is down, time is the most important element in caring for your venison.

Equipment

It's an unusual quirk that many hunters invest prodigious amounts of time in deciding upon various equipment items that have absolutely nothing to do with the handling of their game meat, then almost as an afterthought reach for just any knife when it's time to perform some cutting chore or another.

This is regrettable because there are innumerable knife designs and sizes, each intended for given tasks. By taking advantage of at least several models, the hunter, like the master mechanic with many different tools, can enjoy far more versatility and efficiency in performing sundry cutting chores.

The five times a deer hunter is likely to need a knife are during field dressing, skinning, caping, rough-butchering, and meat cutting (final reduction of various cuts into freezer-ready portions). In most of these cases, distinctly different knife sizes and blade designs are sure to prove superior to others. Some are even mutually exclusive. A skinning knife, for example, calls for a wide, upswept or backswept blade, the round cutting edge thereby suiting the sweeping or rotary stroke used in hide removal. A caping knife must be small, slender, and acutely pointed for working in very tight places. Knives for boning, butchering, or slicing meat, on the other hand, should be much longer and straight-bladed.

In the realm of field dressing knives, although many models may be suitable for this particular operation, "short and light" are sound principles to abide by. Indeed, it's almost a truism that the more experienced a hunter becomes over the years, the shorter grow his knife blades. Friend and professional big-game guide, Bill Tomlinson, who works out of Boise, Idaho, commonly relies upon a stockman's knife with a mere two-inch blade for dressing out most of his deer. Throughout the Rocky Mountain states, in fact, it's becoming almost faddish for outfitters to pull some dainty little thing out of their pockets, set to the task of dressing their deer, and often, to the astonishment of their less-accomplished clients, do a very commendable job.

If all of this sounds like nothing more than showboating, consider that a surgeon, who requires the ultimate precision in his cutting chores, uses a scalpel with a blade a mere one and one-quarter inch in length. Of course, it's not necessary for the average deer hunter to go to such extremes to demonstrate his knife-handling prowess. But the point to be made is, absolutely forget about long, saber-type knives, especially those reminiscent of the Bowie genre or similar ones that look better suited to cutting sugar cane than field dressing deer. These tools, sheath ridden and sagging down almost to one's knee, have little practical purpose other than making life miserable when getting in and out of a vehicle, squatting down into a narrow tree-stand seat or sneaking through brush-cover.

The bottom line is that any manner of venison cutting, including field dressing, can be somewhat delicate at times and requires a bit of finesse if the final product is to have a neat, pleasing, well-manicured appearance. Yet with a knife possessing a blade much more than four inches in length, your wrist and fingers find themselves too far away from the actual cutting site to accurately control the blade.

As to cutting-edge design, straight, trailing-point and drop-point blades are the three most commonly preferred for field dressing; while I personally prefer drop-point blades, there is no advantage to being a conformist. Pick the one you enjoy using most and can handle with the greatest dexterity. This might be a fixed-blade sheath knife, a mid-size folder that goes into your pocket, or a slightly larger folder that rides in a belt pouch.

There was a time many years ago when I was a fan of blades made of relatively soft carbon steel such as C-1095 because I could easily hone them razor sharp. Then, during the course of field dressing, all that was necessary was taking an occasional swipe across a whetstone to touch it up a bit. Now, I'm no longer content with such knives but prefer those of much harder steel that hold their edges through the duration of most cutting chores. Typically, this means a blade made from stainless-steel alloy or high carbon steel. These knives can be awesomely difficult to sharpen if the hunter neglects them for prolonged periods. But otherwise, their edge-holding ability is impressive and allows the hunter to leave his whetstone in camp or at home, thereby eliminating just one more item bulging his already overloaded pockets.

In addition to the knife needed for field dressing, there are a few other minor essentials a deer hunter will need minutes after the deer is down. One often forgotten item is a long, rectangular plastic bag for the liver and heart. I recommend two discarded bread wrappers, one slipped inside the other for added strength. They're free and perfectly suited to a unique trick I devised long ago for removing these meat cuts from the field; more on this later. A foot-long length of common cotton string is important. Include several paper towels and a moist towelette in a sealed packet for clean-up chores afterward.

Field Dressing Myths

There is clearly no other aspect of deer hunting more riddled with misconceptions than the proper field care of deer. Even many of those who salute the flag every morning, have wheat germ for breakfast, and help little old ladies cross the street all too commonly become villains when it comes to field care of their deer.

We're all products of our accumulated learning experiences, and when a young hunter is taught by his or her father that a deer's tarsal glands must first be removed to prevent the venison from tasting gamey, why should the young hunter believe otherwise?

So let's first dispense with several fables that may actually do more harm than good.

The tarsal glands–those moist, sticky, dark tufts of hair surrounding inch-long gland slits located just below the knee on each rear hock–cease functioning when a deer dies. And since they are situated a good distance from the prime venison of other body parts, there is no way for them to adversely affect the meat if you merely leave them alone.

Whenever the tarsal gland's musk does indeed taint the meat, it's always due to one reason: an ill-informed hunter hacked away at the glands with his knife and then used the same knife, without cleaning the blade, to perform other cutting work and thus transferred the pungent tarsal scent to other parts of the carcass.

I once watched in dismay as a hunter feverishly attempted to remove the tarsal glands of a mule deer. By the time he was finished, sticky gland-scent

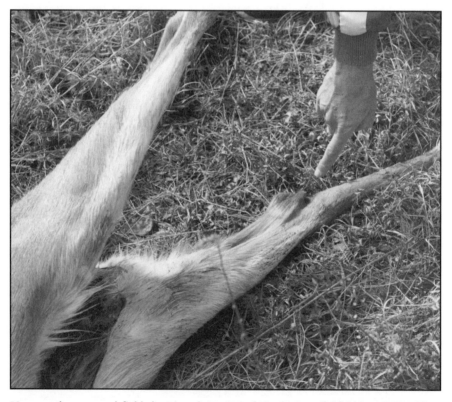

Many myths surround field dressing deer, one of the longest-held being the need to remove the tarsal glands. Just leave them alone and they'll do no harm; trouble arises only when a hunter begins cutting at them and transfers their oily scent to his hands and knife blade.

stains randomly adorned the front of his jeans, one sleeve of his shirt, and both hands. His knife blade verily dripped of the stuff. Next he quartered the meat, handling much of it against his clothing as he stuffed it into game sacks. I'll bet that venison tasted like turpentine.

Nor is there any logical reason for cutting the deer's throat in some misguided belief that it's necessary to bleed the animal. What blood it does not lose on the ground moments after the shot will pump quickly into the chest cavity. You'll notice this when you open the deer and the stuff literally pours out.

Cutting open the animal's neck region accomplishes only two things. It ruins the hide, and right then and there cancels any plans you might have later to send your deer to a taxidermist. It also creates an unnecessary entrance into the body cavity through which blowflies, dirt, and other contaminants may enter and cause the beginning stages of spoilage.

Yet another horrendous practice I've witnessed on many occasions is opening up a deer from stem to stern. What I mean is, after making an abdominal incision, the hunter continues cutting all the way through the chest, bearing down on his knife handle to cut through the sternum and ribs, then continuing yet onward until he reaches the base of the lower jaw. After that, he about-faces, reaches for an axe, and literally does a hatchet job on the deer's pelvis.

Opening the chest region in such a manner again unnecessarily exposes too much meat to contamination. Attempting to split the pelvic arch, which professional butchers call the Aitch bone, chiefly results in the bladder being punctured, the hindquarter roasts being at least superficially damaged, and jagged splinters of bone telling all the world of the hunter's ineptness.

The right way, when a deer is down, involves just two fundamental considerations. The first is reducing the temperature of the carcass in order to cool all those precious steaks and roasts until such time as they are secured in wrapped packages ready for the freezer. The second concern is all the while keeping the meat clean and free of contaminants by dirt or insects.

Incidentally, whitetails, mule deer, and blacktails are anatomically identical. There are only minor differences in the coloration of their body hair, the size of their tails, and the basic configuration of their antler-structure. So everything said in this book about field dressing "deer," rough-butchering, and final meat-cutting techniques, and even the recipes, apply equally to all of the various subspecies.

By the Numbers

The easiest field-dressing procedure we've found is as follows:

1. To keep the animal and your work area as clean as possible, roll the deer onto its back, with its head and upper chest region on slightly higher ground.

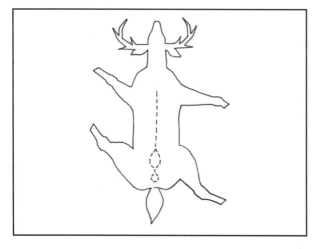

This is the only incision necessary to remove a deer's insides in order to begin rapidly cooling the meat; if the incision is lengthened any further toward the neck, you'll ruin the cape for taxidermy purposes.

Taking a minute to do this before opening the animal's body cavity will allow its insides, particularly the accumulated blood, to flow out and downhill, away from the carcass.

2. Straddle the deer, facing the head, and make an abdominal incision by grasping between your thumb and forefinger a clump of belly hair and lifting. Simultaneously, use just the tip of your knife blade to slice a small starter hole about two inches in length. This should allow you to insert the first two fingers of your left hand, palm facing up.

3. Next, slightly spread those two fingers and lift them upward. Then, between your spread fingers, insert just the forward inch of your knife blade, edge facing up, and guide the blade from the base of the reproductive organs

Begin by rolling the animal onto its back and opening the abdominal region, working in the direction of the chest. It's a great help to have a partner to hold the legs and steady the carcass.

up the centerline of the animal to the sternum (the breastbone, just where the ribs begin).

The reason for lifting the abdominal wall and using the knife with the blade edge facing up is to ensure that you do not inadvertently slice into the intestines lying directly below and cause messy digestive matter to spill all over.

4. As the abdominal incision is completed, the paunch and intestines will begin to bulge up and out. You can now set your knife aside briefly and pull them most of the remainder of the way out of the body cavity with your hands until you come to the diaphragm. This is a sheetlike wall of thin skin inside the body cavity that separates the lower intestinal organs from those

The incision should go only to the sternum, no farther. If a partner is not available to help, steady the carcass by bracing the back of your leg against the animal's leg.

higher up in the chest region. Use your knife to cut the diaphragm free by running the blade around the entire inside perimeter of the chest cavity to expose the lungs and heart.

5. The next step is equally easy but just a tad messy, so take off your wrist watch and roll up your sleeves, as you'll be inserting your arms full length up into the chest cavity.

With the abdominal organs lying on the ground beside the deer, yet still attached to the pelvic region, extend one arm up into the chest cavity to the base of the neck and feel for the windpipe and esophagus. These will feel like

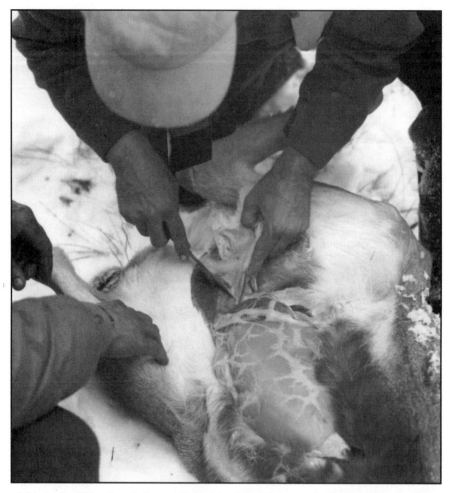

The paunch will begin to bulge up and can be pulled out with the hands, with only minor cuts necessary to free it from restraining ligaments. Then make a shallow cut around the reproductive organs and remove them.

two tubes, a soft, three-quarter-inch-diameter tube lying on top of a rigid, one and one-half-inch-diameter ribbed tube. Grasp the twin-tube assembly with one hand, then insert your knife (very carefully) with the other hand and sever the tubes as high up in the neck as you can reach.

Withdraw the knife-holding hand and, still grasping the tubes with the other hand, begin pulling backward. As you continue pulling, the esophagus and windpipe will easily tear from their thin attachments; the heart and lungs will come with them. Pull them free of the body cavity, making just a few judicious cuts here and there if necessary.

6. Sever the heart from its various restraining ligaments and set it aside on clean grass, moss, or ferns to cool and drain. Then do the same with the

liver, which is attached to the intestines from the abdominal region. Still another myth pertains to removing a deer's gall bladder; humans have one, attached to their liver, but deer don't; hence, there is none to remove.

7. When you began field dressing, you were straddling the deer, facing the head. Now, turn around and face the opposite direction to begin removing the remainder of the lower intestines and the reproductive/excretory tract.

Extend your shallow abdominal cut to the base of the penis (or, if it's a doe, make a shallow, oval cut around the udder and remove that flap of skin). Since the penis and testicles lie on top of the abdomen, they're easily removed. Lift the penis gently and simply slice the skin around both sides of the organ, taking as little skin as possible, as this protects the valuable hindquarter meat lying on either side. Continue lifting and cutting, next going around the testicles; where the penis tube enters the bladder cavity there is a bit of soft cartilage you can cut with your knife to increase your work area, but be careful not to puncture the bladder lying directly underneath.

Now use your short length of string to tie the urethra (the urine tube) so you can cut the penis and testicles entirely free and discard them without urine from the bladder spraying all over.

8. As you finally go around both sides of the testicles, your two knife cuts will briefly join together again, but an inch farther toward the rear they will have to separate once again, this time to go entirely around the anus.

9. Now turn around and face the opposite direction, toward the head again, and go around the anus with just the tip of your knife blade to make a very shallow cut.

This will create a flap of skin around the diameter of the orifice that you can grab with your fingertips, allowing you to gradually cut deeper and deeper into the pelvic canal to free the rectum, just like coring an apple. Exposing this area is easier if a friend pulls back on the hind legs to lift the rump area a bit; if alone, push back the legs with your left shoulder.

However, the deeper you go into the pelvic canal, cutting the rectum free, the closer you approach the bladder. Care must be taken to not slice into it or you'll have a flood of urine gushing all over. This is one reason why so many expert hunters prefer field dressing with knife blades no longer than four inches; a limited blade length prevents them from going too deeply and perhaps rupturing the bladder.

10. When you reach the point in which the rectum has been entirely encircled and cut free as deep as you can go, stop working from this direction and begin coming in the remainder of the way from the other (abdominal) side.

Gently push away as much lower intestine as possible with one hand, while with the other holding your knife begin to carefully separate the bladder from inside the pelvic canal. Usually, the bladder is a small, soft, pouchlike affair only partially filled with urine and therefore presents no

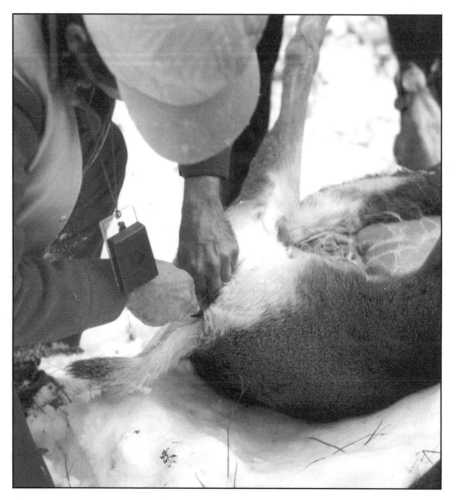

The excretory tract is removed from the pelvic region by coring it like an apple and then pulling the freed matter back through the pelvic cavity.

problem. But if it seems quite full and distended, good advice is pinch the urethra tightly closed with your fingertips just below the string tie. Then cut the string, aim the urethra away from your work area and, exerting gentle hand pressure on the bladder, direct the urine spray away from your work area. Now re-tie the urethra and gently continue cutting the bladder from within the pelvic canal. Soon, cuts made from this direction will meet those previously made from the anus side and you'll be able to pull out the entire reproductive/excretory tract in one long, undamaged string.

All of this may seem quite involved but many hunters can field-dress their deer in the time it takes to read this chapter.

If the weather is cool, you'll now see steam rising from the body cavity, a sure sign your venison is beginning to rapidly cool.

Final Chores

Many hunters merely field-dress their deer in the above manner and that is that. But if you keep in mind that the growth of bacteria is the number-one cause of meat spoilage, and that moisture is the breeding ground for bacteria, you'll immediately recognize the importance of attending to several other matters.

With the deer's insides entirely removed, flop the animal over onto its belly with the animal's front and rear legs spread-eagled and the head slightly uphill. Now grab the antlers and begin vigorously shaking the carcass while slowly dragging it forward several yards.

When you look at the ground, you'll be amazed to see large pools of clotted blood and lymph fluids that you initially thought were released from the body during field dressing, but weren't. Most of this has drained from the upper chest and neck cavities and if they had been left in the deer, bacterial growth would have begun almost immediately. Now, flip the carcass back over onto its back again and use handfuls of clean, dry grass, ferns, or moss to further swab out the entire body cavity, including the abdominal region and excretory tract, to mop up any remaining surface moisture. Then use your paper toweling and moistened towelette to clean your hands and knife.

It is imperative that you remove your deer from the field as soon as possible, so that still other attention can be given the carcass back in camp, even if it means dragging your deer by flashlight. If there is some compelling reason that prevents this until the following morning, don't merely leave your deer laying on its side where the mostly closed body cavity will immediately begin acting like a pressure-cooker.

Lay the deer on its back, propped against a log or rock so it won't roll back over onto its side, and widely spread the abdominal walls with a couple of sticks. Then smile smugly when you see body steam rising from the carcass, indicating that cooling has begun.

If there's a chance that birds or coyotes may begin damaging the carcass during my absence, I usually hang my T-shirt, which is well-fermented after a day's hunt, from a nearby branch; the combination of human odor, and the cloth fluttering in the breeze, will ward away even the most desperate scavengers.

By the way, if you have to leave your deer in the field overnight, it's wise to drag it a short distance so that it's left on a north-facing slope of terrain or at least in a thick stand of conifers. The cooler temperature there, plus the shade, will protect your deer from midmorning sunlight if you're somewhat delayed in returning the following day. Of course, this may not be a critical consideration in cold weather, but south of the Mason-Dixon line it's advice worth heeding.

Finally, it's still necessary to attend to the heart and liver. If the deer is to be left in the field overnight, or while you briefly return to camp to enlist friends to help with the dragging-out effort, simply place the organs in your plastic bag and carry them back to camp. But if you decide to begin immediately dragging your deer, here is the plastic bag trick I mentioned earlier.

A bag containing the liver and heart is a bit too heavy and bulky to put in your coat pocket, and you can't easily carry it because you need both hands free for dragging the animal.

Place the bag inside the chest cavity. Next, twist the long tail of the bread wrapper and poke it out the bullet hole through the ribs in the lung region. On the outside, grab the visible tail, pull on it until the liver/heart bag inside is snug against the rib cage, then tie a large knot in the tail on the outside of the hide. Your liver and heart will now ride out of the woods inside the body cavity of the deer, protected from dirt and grime.

4

Bringing Your Deer Out

T he act of getting a buck out of the woods and back to one's
parked vehicle, camp, or home seems to perennially be riddled
with misinformation. It's logical to assume that dragging a deer
requires only a strong back and weak mind. But since I've
always been adverse to hard work, I've tried every conceivable
way of transporting deer in the hopes of lucking upon small tricks that might
make life easier. Much of what I tried in earlier years didn't work very well.

One ludicrous idea that never fails to appear in sportsmen's magazines
every year is a sketch of two hunters carrying a deer that is trussed upside-
down to a long pole they've lifted and are carrying on their shoulders. What
I learned is that the high center of gravity of the deadweight mass will cause
the carcass to shift and sway around. The end result of that bouncing weight
is hunters arriving back in camp with back pains and shoulders rubbed raw.

There is only one situation in which I recommend this or the similar
procedure of carrying a deer on a stretcher-like affair between two poles.

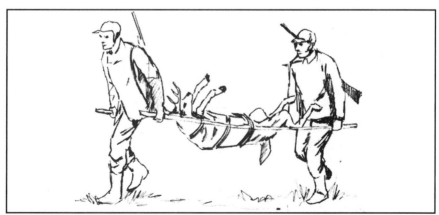

The only time the animal should be lifted and bodily carried is when there is standing
water and swampy terrain. Don't use a single log carried high on your shoulders as
sometimes depicted in sportsmen's magazines. Instead, use two sticks to fashion a
stretcher-like affair to lower the deer's center of gravity.

That's when a deer is killed far back in swampy habitat and must be bodily lifted and carried to avoid being dragged through water and black muck.

A simple variation of the stretcher-carry is making a travois so that the lower part of the animal's weight is on the ground.

The most common method used by hunters is simply grabbing the deer's antlers with one hand or the other and dragging the animal across the ground. Although the practice is widespread, words of precaution are in order.

The most common method of removing a deer from the field is to simply grab the antlers and begin dragging. But there are better ways that are safer and easier on the body.

If the drag is a long one, and one's youth slipped away many sunsets ago, all kinds of back and shoulder problems may ensue. The reason for this is that the dead weight of the animal on the ground presents a very low center of gravity, requiring the hunter to bend low to grab onto it and remain in his crouched position through the duration of the drag. This results in tremendous strain upon both the vertebral column and its contiguous musculature, often causing you to remember the dragging experience far longer than you would have liked. Also, should you slip on wet leaves or snowpack, there's at least a fair possibility of pointed antler tines going into your calf muscles.

Sensible Methods That Work

One technique is no more complicated than using a short length of rope and a stick of wood that's about two inches in diameter by two feet in length.

First raise the deer's front hooves and place them behind the antlers (or behind the ears if it's a doe) and lash them to the neck so they are up and out of the way, eliminating their resistance against the ground and giving you a somewhat pointed object to pull through the cover.

Next, tie the other end of the rope to the center of the stick and begin wrapping it around until it's about two feet from the deer's head. At this time, take a half-hitch around the stick with the rope so it won't unwind.

Now place your hands behind your back, one holding either side of the drag stick, lift the head and front shoulders of the deer slightly off the ground, and begin heading for camp. Compared to grabbing onto the antlers and heaving-ho, this method allows you to stand almost at full height while dragging. And since there is about a one and one-half foot distance from your backside to the antlers, there's little chance of them ever gouging you.

Ideally, the best thing is using this drag method with a partner, each grabbing onto one side of the stick. It is amazing how easy this makes the job, especially if you have gloves to protect your hands. When your right hand and arm get tired (your partner will be on the opposite side, using his left hand and arm), stop to catch your breath and then switch places for a while.

This is the recommended method of removing a deer from the field if the required dragging distance is just a few hundred yards or if most of the route is downhill. If it's a longer drag, or if it will take you uphill, there are easier methods.

One is using some type of shoulder harness. Many varieties are available in sporting-goods stores and through hunting mail-order catalogs like Cabela's and RedHead/Bass Pro Shops. Most have the same type of webbed seat-belt material used in vehicles. And some of the more common types have a belt that buckles around the waist, or a diagonal shoulder strap with a longer strap or rope going off the backside that is tied to the deer's head.

A short, stout length of branch is an easy way to drag deer across flat terrain.

If the drag is a relatively long distance, and part of it is uphill, a shoulder harness allows the back and shoulder muscles to bear most of the workload.

Not too long ago I tested one of these devices by dragging a heavy log around my backyard and found the going surprisingly easy. Then, later in the season, I archery-killed a fat doe and found the dragging easier still. I was pleased as punch, until the following year when I killed a buck and ran into all kinds of difficulties. The antlers kept digging into the ground or grabbing roots and brush, continually jerking me to a sudden halt.

Then I had a brainstorm. Why not drag the deer by its hind legs instead of its head, so brush and other obstacles would slide right over the natural curvatures of the rack? It works great, with one exception. Since you're dragging the carcass against the grain of the hair, the hide will be ruined.

A somewhat different gizmo is called the Deer Drag. This affair consists of a length of heavy-duty aircraft cable and a comfortable rubber handle that is not hard on the hands. Just slip the cable noose over the head or antlers, snug it up a bit, and when you begin dragging, the short length of cable is designed to lift the head and neck of the animal off the ground.

The Peter Fiduccia Lifetime Deer Drag is a safe drag to use and easy to carry. This handle-type deer drag, with a short length of cable around the base of the antlers, makes short work of getting deer out of the woods. Available from Whitetail Strategies at www.deerdoctor.com.

Still Better Ideas

It's been said that everyone achieves a fleeting moment of fame at least once in his life. And for Jim Matthews of Duluth, Minnesota, that brief moment involved a common sheet of plastic.

As a taxidermist, Matthews wanted to make a full-body mount of a deer for his studio. This meant somehow getting his deer out of the woods without dragging it on the ground and scuffing up the hide.

"If you place the plastic on the ground, lay the deer on top, and then wrap the plastic around the carcass and tie it with cord before you begin dragging, you'll be amazed," Matthews explained. "The slick-surfaced plastic reduces ground friction against the hide by at least fifty percent."

Hearing this, I wasn't surprised the following year when a Wisconsin company introduced the Deer Sleigh'r, available through mail-order hunting catalogs. The Deer Sleigh'r improves upon Matthews' idea because it's made of a special heavy-duty plastic that won't tear when dragged over sharp rocks and brush. I tried it that season and found I could easily drag a one hundred eighty-pound animal with just one hand. Moreover, if it's a drag of a mile or more, the gizmo can easily be towed behind a four-wheeler.

Making Hard Work Easy

When dragging a deer by any method, take it slow and easy, particularly if you're over forty years old. Pace yourself. Stop every fifty yards or so, even if you do not feel overly tired. This rest time allows you to scout ahead a bit for the easiest drag route. In this manner you can find and then take advantage of slight variations in the terrain, avoiding even short uphill drags and following the best trail to skirt rock formations, blowdowns, or other obstacles.

It's usually best to take a slightly longer route if it enables you to stay on level ground or drag downhill. I've even been known to briefly drag my deer in the opposite direction of camp if it means eventually coming to dry, powdery snow, damp leaves, pine needles, or some other terrain surface that allows the remainder of the drag to see the deer carcass effortlessly slide along.

When hunting alone, I like to use the leap-frog method to simultaneously bring out my deer and the hunting equipment I was using that day. Simply drag the deer fifty yards, stop, then go back and pick up your rifle or bow, portable stand, heavy outer coat, and any other gear. and carry the stuff fifty yards beyond the animal. Then return to the deer and drag it up to where the gear is.

This change of pace makes deer dragging far less tiring. But also, you can do a bit of scouting for the easiest drag route and move aside any dead branches or other obstacles that may be blocking the route as you're carrying your equipment forward.

Better still is when there are three or four hunters in the group. Two can begin dragging the deer. The third carries all the rifles and day packs. The fourth works farther ahead, finding the best trail and pushing aside debris. Then, every two hundred yards or so, they alternate positions.

Horse-Packing Your Deer

In most situations, a hunter who has successfully collected his deer will find he's within relatively easy dragging distance of a road or trail. This is typically the case when whitetail hunting east of the Mississippi. There are some situations, however, in which whitetails are taken in remote back-country places, especially in the northern border states, Canadian provinces, and in many Rocky Mountain states where they often coexist with mule deer and elk.

In such cases, dragging a deer all the way to camp or a vehicle may be impossible, and this leaves only three choices. You'll probably not seriously consider the first option, hiring a helicopter to fly in and hover overhead while dropping a cable down to you and your deer. Don't laugh. I heard of a multi-millionaire computer programmer, who works for Microsoft, who does that very thing every year.

The other alternatives–far more realistic approaches–are using either your back or a horse's back to transport your venison.

Removing a deer by horseback is possible In many deer-hunting situations. Ranchers who live near popular hunting regions commonly offer this service for hire.

The easiest, of course, is leading a packhorse to camp with your deer meat aboard. Most hunters obviously don't own horses (or mules), but in those regions where they are most likely to be needed for hunting work they are widely available for rental. Check the Yellow Pages of a local phone book, the classified ads in local newspapers, or ask the nearest rancher.

Even though horses or mules may not be playing a daily role in your hunting activities, it's wise to learn in advance which ranchers in your hunting area have them available. Most likely you'll be able to navigate your four-wheel-drive truck or ATV close to the kill site and retrieve your deer by dragging it the remaining distance. But it's nice to know where you can obtain four-footed help in bringing out your animal, if your deer runs into upside-down real estate before dropping, or if you sprain your ankle.

Rarely do ranchers simply hire out horses or mules and let strangers drive away with them in transport trailers. It's standard practice that when you rent a horse or mule, you also hire the owner or one of his hired hands for a few hours; that individual knows how to bridle the animal, which types of saddles or pack carriers to use and how to cinch them in place, how to load and distribute the game meat, how to control the animal, and all the rest. It will cost more than just a couple of bucks to remove your deer from the hinterland in this manner, but at the same time you save worry, hassle, and mistakes because the person hired assumes the responsibility of getting your precious venison cargo and antlers back to where you can resume caring for it yourself.

Get a Faux Horse or Mule

Although a live horse or mule does a yeoman's job of removing a deer from the field, we've seen how they involve pre-planning and a good deal of expense. A neat substitute are two items my friend Ray McIntyre conceived. Called The Horse and The Mule, they are far from being hay-burners.

McIntyre is the head man of Warren & Sweat, the company that makes premium tree stands, and his latest brainstorms are carryalls fitted with one or two small bicycle wheels that can be pushed or pulled to transport deer across even fairly rugged terrain. The Horse's unique design places the weight over the axle, producing almost zero pounds at the handle, allowing one man to simultaneously transport two large deer if necessary. The Mule is designed for transporting one deer and is especially well-suited for use in snow and swamps, and goes over logs and rocks with ease.

Backpacking Your Deer

In situations in which horses (either real or mechanical) are not available, or cannot be used due to the inhospitable nature of the terrain, you must

Two-wheeled carryalls are popular with many hunters. They'll carry a heavy load and are best suited for level terrain where there is not much cover blocking the route.

Hunters who frequently find their quarry in steep or rugged terrain prefer a single-wheel carryall for efficiently removing their deer from the field.

become the beast of burden yourself and carry the deer out on your back. This is why I always have the following items in camp or back in my vehicle: a lightweight, tubular backpack frame, several muslin gamebags, a twenty-foot length of thin nylon lashing cord, a heavy-duty folding knife with a small saw blade in its housing, and a canteen of water. Seldom are these ever needed on an average deer hunt, but when the fateful day arrives, as it eventually will, they're more than worth any inconvenience of having them along.

After field dressing your deer, and with it now laying on its back with its body cavity propped open to allow cooling, hike back to your vehicle to get your packing-out essentials. This allows you to carry out the liver and heart on that first trip and to simultaneously relieve yourself of your rifle, binoculars, and other gear no longer needed that day. You can also exchange your heavy outerwear for lighter-weight garments; just be sure you continue to wear your orange vest.

After returning to the kill site, use your knife's saw blade to remove the deer's four lower legs at the knee joint; this will lighten the overall carcass weight by ten pounds.

Next, cut the head off at the base of the neck where it joins the main body torso. This load, depending upon the weight of the antlers, will probably be around forty pounds.

Finally, cut the deer into two equal halves; the front half will weigh about forty pounds and the back half about fifty pounds. This leaves three relatively easy packloads to carry out.

The only disadvantage to packing out a deer in this manner, other than the physical work involved, is that the hide must be sacrificed. Although the hide could be entirely removed from the carcass before cutting it into three sections, I prefer to leave it attached to serve as protection for the venison. Each carcass section is then slipped into its muslin gamebag to further protect the venison from trail grime and insects, especially where the hide has been cut and meat has been exposed.

A few other tips are also worth passing on. If the weather permits, it's wise to leave the field-dressed deer at the kill site until the following morning before reducing it to backpacking sizes. The cold night air will rigidly firm up the meat, making it easier to handle than when it's warm and soft. Obviously, temperatures warmer than 50°F during midday precludes this approach; when it's hot you'll want to get your venison back to camp as quickly as possible.

Also, when lashing down the large carcass sections on the packframe, take whatever time is necessary to balance the heavy load. You don't want to find yourself carrying a lopsided load, as this invites losing one's balance and falling, or possibly spraining an ankle on the greater weight-bearing foot.

In the most rugged terrain, the only option may be to bring out your deer piecemeal by first reducing it to quarters at the field dressing site and then lashing them to a packframe.

Try to distribute the meat evenly, so it is shoving straight down on the centerline of the packframe.

Also try to position the weight as high as possible (within reason) on the packframe. This will allow you to maintain a normal upright stance while hiking, rather than being hunched over. The advantage here, particularly if you have a waist belt on your packframe, is that your hips and strong upper leg regions can help bear the brunt of the weighty load rather than your back alone having the entire responsibility.

5

Camp Care of Deer Meat

O utside your mountain cabin the dark chill of night is beginning to settle like a shroud over the landscape and sparkles of frost are littering the ground like bits of broken glass. The wind is howling ominously and there are spits of sleet in the air. But at this moment nothing could dampen your spirits, for only a dozen paces from the front door a single handsome buck hangs from a birch limb in testimony to your hunting skills and hard work. It's the first deer to arrive in camp and you're both proud and satisfied that you've earned every ounce of your winter's supply of venison.

So spend the evening celebrating, but bear in mind that your deer is going to require a good bit of attention during upcoming days. You'll want to ensure that the venison remains cool and protected from flying and crawling marauders, and you'll want to clean the carcass for the trip home. Your mind is buzzing with things to remember and steps to follow. But now is the moment to throw another log on the fire, graciously accept another handshake, and sip once more from your hot mug.

A hanging deer makes a happy camp; many hunters prefer to hang their deer from the head.
(photo by Tom Slinsky)

Hanging Your Deer

As soon as deer have been transported back to camp they are traditionally hung from some type of overhead device. I prefer a stout tree limb because little work is involved compared to building a horizontal meatpole of sorts. Also, if it's still early in the season and the weather is warm, leaves on the trees will shade your animal carcass from the bright sunlight.

Whatever the design of the hanging mechanisms, however, their purposes are all the same: namely, to get the animal up and off the ground so it can be worked upon, so the carcass will remain clean of dirt, so ground-crawling critters won't bother it, and so air can circulate to facilitate cooling.

Visit almost any camp and you'll see many deer hanging by their heads while others are hanging by the hind legs, their owners claiming the matter is no more than personal preference.

There are several reasons why I prefer hanging deer by the hind legs. With the carcass in this position, remaining body heat is free to rise and easily escape. Conversely, if you hang a deer by the antlers, rising body heat will find itself trapped inside the chamberlike chest cavity, actually caus-

The author prefers to hang a deer from the back legs instead of the head. This allows body heat to quickly escape from the carcass so the venison can begin to rapidly cool.

ing the upper half of the carcass to begin slightly warming up again!

Also, the greatest quantity of a deer's blood, lymph, and other body fluids are located in the front half of the body. Most of these fluids have been removed during earlier field dressing activities, but there's still some remaining in the deer's smaller veins and arteries and throughout tiny pockets and intra-muscular spaces. When the animal is hung, these body fluids, like all liquids, will begin to slowly drain to the lowest elevation they can find. This is all to the good, but you'll want them to exit the carcass as quickly as possible, not slowly seep down over and through the carcass and perhaps invite the growth of bacterial spoilage or impart the venison with objectionable flavors.

If you'll recall, during field dressing operations the windpipe and esophagus were severed high up in the neck region. Therefore, if the deer is hung by the hind legs, any residual body fluids wanting to drain away will simply follow a short, downhill course through the now-wide-open windpipe/

esophagus region and quickly pass out through the nostrils and mouth without contacting any valuable cuts of meat. In fact, a day or two later you'll notice a puddle of the stuff on the ground directly beneath the animal's head.

To hang a deer by the hind legs, first make a two-inch-long slit with a knife through the thin skin separating the hock of each rear leg from the Achilles tendon. Then insert the opposite ends of a gambrel through these two holes, tie a rope to its top center, and hoist the deer aloft. Gambrels all serve the same function but vary somewhat in design; they're available through hunting mail-order catalogs and at farm-supply stores.

Hanging a deer by the hind legs requires the use of some type of gambrel inserted horizontally through the Achilles tendons. Be sure to hang your deer higher than you ordinarily might if there are coyotes or free-roaming dogs in the region. (photo by New Hampshire Game & Fish)

Actually lifting the deer off the ground is most commonly done with the help of partners, using the Armstrong method. But if alone, a miniature block and tackle makes the work a breeze, as does fashioning a pulley to the overhead tree limb and pulling on the lift-rope with a vehicle or ATV.

There are many ways to lift your deer off the ground. The Armstrong Method, with the help of several partners, is the most common. You can also use an ATV or pickup. If it's a one-man operation, you can't beat a small block and tackle made for the purpose.

Initial Meat-Care Procedures

At this point I'm going to discuss various venison-care activities every hunter must attend to sooner or later. The sequence in which these tasks are performed may vary, depending upon average daily air temperatures, prevailing weather conditions, and so on.

Generally, when my deer arrives in camp, the first order of business, even before hanging the animal, is removing the heart and liver from their plastic bag and placing the two organs in a clean pail filled with water and one cup of salt. It's even wise to cut the liver into two or three large pieces to expose the inside, although this is not necessary with the smaller heart.

Slosh the organ pieces around in the water to remove surface debris, dried blood, and interior blood clots. In a few minutes the water will turn bright red. Dump this water out and add fresh salted water. Rub the liver gently with your hands and poke your fingers inside the large arteries of the heart to further loosen and dislodge blood clots from inside. When the water turns bright red still again, discard it and again replenish the supply with clean salted water.

Now, allow the heart and liver to soak for six to eight hours. This final soaking will thoroughly purge both organs of any remaining traces of blood. If you've never cared for venison liver or heart, perhaps they were never cared for properly in this manner; otherwise, don't leave them in the field because there are sure to be others in camp who would appreciate having them.

After the liver and heart have completed their soaking period, rinse them with clean water and place them on a drainboard for fifteen minutes. Then place them in a plastic bag in your refrigerator or camping cooler. Traditionally, liver and heart are consumed in camp for dinner the first night or the very next morning for breakfast. They can also be properly wrapped and frozen for later use (see Chapter 14), although fresh liver is always superior to that which has been frozen.

At this time, I also like to remove the tenderloin steaks.

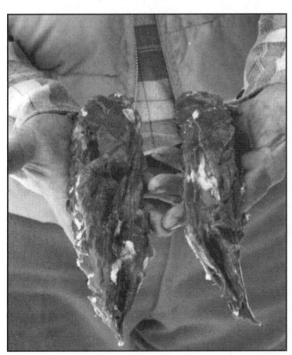

The first venison to be tended to in camp is the heart and liver, which should begin soaking in salt water. Then immediately remove the tenderloins from inside the rib cage; these are the most tender cuts, comparable to a beef's filet mignon.

These should not be confused with the long backstraps located on the exterior of the carcass along either side of the backbone and which require removing the hide to obtain. Rather, they are much smaller, only two inches in diameter by about twelve inches in length, and they are located along both sides of the backbone inside the chest cavity.

I call them mini-tenderloins, but whatever they're called, they are the most tender venison any deer possesses and anatomically are comparable to the filet mignons of beef steers. The easiest way to remove these prime strips of meat is by using a small knife, even a pocketknife, to separate one end or the other from attachments along the backbone and then filleting them the remainder of the way out. When the deer carcass is hanging by the hind legs, with the body cavity open and exposed, removal of the mini-tenderloins is far easier than when the deer is hanging by the head, which prevents you from easily seeing your work.

Strangely, many hunters leave the mini-tenderloins in their deer until they later begin full butchering operations at home, but I advise against this practice. By that time the tenderloins, since they have no protective hide-covering, will have acquired a glaze or hard casing on their exposed surfaces, which must then be trimmed away, resulting in a significant loss of the prime meat. A much better approach is to remove the mini-tenderloins as soon as possible, trim them of bloodied areas and fat, then quickly refrigerate them.

Another thing in favor of removing the mini-tenderloins in camp is to please any partners who dislike liver or heart but would nevertheless like to share in the celebration of eating venison on the eve of the first deer brought into camp.

With the heart, liver, and mini-tenderloins attended to, your next chore is cleaning the deer carcass still hanging outside. Use a small knife to trim away bloodied, unwanted skin and tissue remnants and fat globs surrounding the field-dressing incision and throughout the abdominal and excretory regions; you're not going to eat these anyway, so why allow them to become breeding areas for bacterial contamination that may spoil adjacent meat areas?

If enough water is available, I like to wash out the inside of the body cavity. Many hunters consider this a cardinal sin, claiming water should never be allowed to touch meat or other parts of the carcass, but according to professional butchers this is merely another old wive's tale. Washing, particularly if a bit of salt is dissolved in the water, facilitates the removal of dried blood and other debris that may not have been entirely removed during field dressing or that found its way inside the body cavity when the deer was being dragged out of the woods. Removal of these potential contaminants is imperative if the carcass is to properly age without spoiling. Just remember to use your water sparingly (most of it will drain downward and exit through the nostrils and mouth) and afterwards use clean rags or paper towels to completely blot up any remaining moisture; the ribs should literally shine.

If the deer was backpacked out in large chunks, be sure to trim and clean them as well. A small terrycloth towel soaked in warm water and then wrung out serves nicely. Dried blood that is too stubborn to remove with a damp rag alone will easily come away by occasionally dipping the towel in a small bowl of vinegar.

All of these measures result in a nice deer carcass that is far more presentable and easy to work with at butchering time than one that is dirty and stained with dried blood. That results in far more venison eventually finding its way to your table.

Protecting Your Deer Carcass

Every year, megatons of prime venison is lost due to a variety of unforeseen events. Warm-weather spoilage and infestation by blowflies are the two leading culprits.

Ideally, deer hanging in camp should not be subjected to air temperatures below 25°F at night or higher than 45°F during midday. If either situation is anticipated or arrives without warning, special measures should be taken to prevent the meat from freezing or becoming too warm and spoiling.

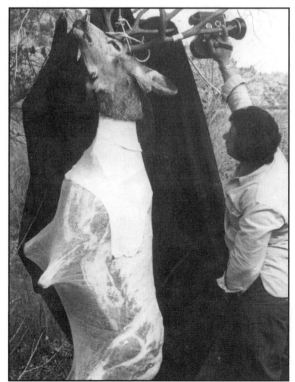

Measures should be taken to prevent the carcass from being exposed to wide temperature ranges. Draping the carcass with a heavy tarp will prevent it from freezing at night. Conversely, in hot weather, draping it during the midday hours will allow the venison to retain the coldness it achieved the previous night.

Begin by hanging the deer in a location that is shaded during the better part of the day. In this manner, the carcass will undergo sufficient chilling during the night hours to keep the meat cool during the daylight hours.

One hunter I know saved an old sleeping bag that had seen years of use; he literally "bags" his deer whenever it's bitter cold. By cutting the bottom edge of the bag open, he doesn't face the problem of trying to slip the deer inside. He merely wraps the bag around the deer and closes the zipper to insulate the venison just enough to prevent it from freezing. He also does this during extremely hot weather, allowing the deer to chill overnight and then, first thing in the morning, wrapping it with the sleeping bag to retain its cool temperature throughout the day. At the end of each hunting trip he merely tosses the bag into his washing machine, so it's clean for next year's outing.

Other hunters who may not want to go to this trouble should at least have a piece of canvas tarpaulin in camp that can be draped over their hanging deer to prevent it from freezing or being exposed to warm midday temperatures.

Blowflies are the bane of deer hunters. They look like common houseflies but with metallic bluish or greenish colors, and as soon as the daytime temperatures rise into the upper thirties they'll swarm to your deer's hanging location. They enact their dastardly deeds by landing on exposed meat and laying thousands of tiny white eggs. In two or three days, the eggs hatch into larvae that feed upon the meat. By the time a hunter first notices blowflies on his deer, much of the venison may already have to be sacrificed. Consequently, strict measures must be taken at the outset to prevent the flies from ever touching your deer. In warm states throughout the South and Southwest, hunters construct special deer-hanging houses to protect their deer. The buildings resemble outhouses in size but have screened walls, with an overhead roof to shelter hanging deer from inclement weather, and are permanent affairs in annual deer camps.

In hunting situations in which building such structures would be inconvenient or even prohibited, other remedies must be sought.

First, forget the old advice about sprinkling the carcass with pepper. You'll need five pounds of the stuff to cover every square inch; otherwise flies will land in the many tiny places not coated, and there will be countless such places because breezes will blow much of it away.

Gamebags, on the other hand, do an excellent job of protecting deer carcasses from blowflies and other insects, provided they are the right kind and used properly. Don't cheap-out and buy the one dollar cheesecloth gamebags found in many sporting-goods stores. Their thin, fragile, wide-mesh construction is about as effective in warding away insects as waving your arms and cursing.

To protect a hanging deer from insects such as blowflies, which can ruin venison in short order, wise hunters invest in a special gamebag made for the purpose. To help keep deer clear, gambags can also be used when transporting deer on vehicles.

What you want are heavy-duty gamebags made of porous but tightly woven cotton or muslin. They're shaped like long tubes with a drawstring closure at one end to entirely enclose the carcass in a cocoon. Such bags cost as much as twenty-five dollars (ouch!), but they do the job well and can be washed and reused for many years.

Three final notes. Don't assume that mere chilly weather means the absence of insects; only if it's below freezing is your venison safe from the critters. Don't assume that leaving the hide on the animal will protect it from insects; there are many entrance points they can use to gain access to your venison. Do make a point of checking your hanging carcass several times each day so you can quickly employ any remedies that may suddenly become necessary. The best game bags on the market are made by The Real McCoy, P.O. Box 726, Crossville, TN 38557 or call (931) 788-6141.

6

Getting Your Deer Home

One time I found myself racing against the clock to save a deer carcass. I was 1,800 miles from home and had taken a nice buck in central Montana, at about 6,000 feet elevation. Since the average daily air temperature was 20°F, I'd become so preoccupied with measures to prevent the carcass from freezing that it never occurred to me that I might lose it to heat.

As I began driving down out of the high country I noticed the air temperature getting warmer, and by the time I'd reached 1,000 feet in elevation it was in the mid-fifties. At the first gas station I checked a phone directory hoping to find a local deer processor who could butcher and freeze my deer on short notice, but there were none in the area. So I put on my thinking cap.

The deer laying in the bed of my pickup had only been field-dressed and still had the hide intact, meaning the carcass was well insulated and, fortunately, still very cold.

The experiment I tried involved nothing more complicated than buying three bags of ice. One was shoved far up into the deer's chest cavity/neck region. The second was placed in the abdominal cavity, while the third was laid between the upper hams of the rear legs. Then the entire carcass was covered with a tarpaulin.

During the next two days I replaced the ice six times. And each time, I used the icy-cold

Before you pack your hunting gear for a long-awaited outing, and before you level your sights on that beautiful buck, give some thought as to how you're going to transport 140 pounds of venison home.

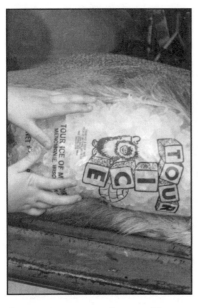

The most convenient transportation method is simply laying the deer carcass in the bed of a pickup. If it's overly warm, insert several ice bags into the body cavity to keep the meat cold.

meltwater from the previous bags to soak the tarpaulin so air rushing through the small pickup-cap's side windows would cause evaporation to aid the cooling effect.

Happily, the 110 pounds of venison cargo made it safely home to Ohio in such good condition that I've since used the same technique on many other outings.

Transporting Deer Short Distances

Clearly, when nature is providing the refrigeration, there's little risk of spoilage by heat. Nevertheless, using recommended transportation techniques is important, because no one wants to pull into his driveway with a disheveled-looking deer covered from hoof to head with dust and road grime.

Although we'll discuss hide removal in another chapter, we should say here that if the hide was removed from the animal in camp, you don't want to expose a naked carcass to highway filth. So leave your deer in its protective gamebag. If you have a second gamebag on hand, use it to double-bag your deer.

The easiest and cleanest way to transport a deer carcass is simply by laying it in the bed of a pickup. But since not everyone owns a pickup, other means have to be considered.

If your vehicle is a car or SUV, and the deer still has its hide, it will serve amply to protect your venison until you arrive home, provided the deer rides as high as possible on your vehicle. Ideally, this means tying the deer onto the roof and, if there is a roof rack, all the better. A rack serves to lift the carcass somewhat, so it is not resting directly on the roof and therefore is at least a bit shielded from heat radiated by the vehicle; what little heat there is, is quickly dissipated by air that circulates beneath and around the carcass.

By the way, never drape your deer carcass over a front fender, as this practice will subject it to both engine heat and road grime thrown into the air by other vehicles ahead of you.

Of late, I've also been using an aluminum equipment carrier made of expandex metal that fits into the trailer-hitch receiver. It's extremely handy but, since it rides low and at the rear of the vehicle, it's necessary to protect the carcass by wrapping it in a tarp; several bungee cords secure the works.

With larger rigs–pickup campers, van conversions, motorhomes, and the like–certain problems arise. These vehicles don't have tailgates for easy loading and their roofs are typically so high off the ground that it's difficult to lift deer up onto them. This tempts many hunters to transport their deer inside on the floor, which isn't wise because the passenger area is generally quite warm. One way to get the deer onto the roof is by backing the vehicle close to the camp meatpole, where the deer is already hanging high, and swinging it sideways onto the roof. Later, at home, back up close to the overhead garage rafters or tree limb where you'll begin butchering operations to easily transfer the deer to the hanging device.

In all of these situations just described, the major concern is not so much keeping the venison cold (Mother Nature is attending to that, or you can do so yourself with ice) but rather keeping the carcass clean.

Camp Butchering the Primal Cuts

For those faraway camps where hunters find themselves in widely fluctuating temperatures, the most convenient solution is to reduce the animal to primal cuts.

By description, primal cuts consist of the four legs, the spine with the backstraps intact, and the neck. The operation can begin almost immediately, but I recommend hanging the deer for at least a day so the carcass can first be cleaned, so that it will naturally purge itself of any residual body fluids, and so that the meat will cool and firm up enough for knife cutting.

Take what happened during a recent hunt in eastern Idaho, where whitetails and mule deer coexist and our group had two of each in camp.

If you're in a cold climate but anticipate driving into hot weather on the trip home, good advice is to semi-butcher your deer in camp.

After each buck had hung for a day, it was duly stripped of its hide. With the temperatures hovering around the zero mark at night, we knew that allowing the deer to hang any longer would result in solidly frozen carcasses, which are no fun to deal with far from home. The venison also suffers.

To semi-butcher a deer, first remove the deer's hide and legs. Then carry the carcass to a makeshift table where final rough-butchering can be done.

We had built a large plywood table in the bed of one of the pickups, with legs fashioned from trunk sections sawed from a dead birch tree. A sheet of heavy-duty plastic covered the makeshift table, held down around the edges with thumbtacks. With the hides and lower legs off the deer, it was easy to transfer each carcass to the clean working surface of the table and further reduce it to primal cuts.

Pre-planning is necessary to partially butcher a deer in camp. We stow a sheet of plywood and roll of heavy plastic with our gear and build a temporary cutting table on-location.

The primal cuts were then loosely wrapped in white freezer paper and placed in camping coolers. Thus protected, the venison would stay very cold without freezing, and at the same time be protected from marauding whiskeyjacks.

Next simply reduce the carcass to primal cuts; that is, front legs, rear legs, saddle, and neck, all of which next go into iced-down camping coolers.

If the trip home is less than twelve hours, the venison will remain in fine condition and need no additional refrigeration. However, if the drive is longer, with an overnight stay along the way, and the air temperature is above 50°F, keep the cooler(s) full of ice. Be sure to lay the wrapped meat on top of the ice (never buried in it), and drain the meltwater from the coolers on a regular basis.

Smaller cuts such as ribs, tenderloins, and backstraps don't have to be meticulously trimmed in camp, either. That work will wait until you get home.

Finally, you'll need a separate cooler if you decide to bring your deer hide home. Good advice is to lay the hide out flat and trim away excess fat and meat, then thoroughly salt the hide. Next, roll (don't fold) the hide into a cylinder and stow it in a heavy-duty plastic garbage bag before placing it

Caring for your hide and neck cape for the trip home is easy. Simply remove all large chunks of fat and other unwanted matter, then liberally rub in salt. Next, roll (never fold) the skin and stow it in a heavy-duty plastic garbage bag.

in the cooler; it will remain in fine condition this way, with no refrigeration needs, for a week or more.

Incidentally, my hunting group's camping coolers never travel empty. Enroute to our hunting destination they hold food; on the trip home they hold venison primal cuts, hides, or, if we're unsuccessful in our hunting efforts, dirty clothes.

Full Butchering in Camp

There are other options available to the hunter far from home who wants to ensure that his venison undergoes safe transportation. When deer hunting in various western states, for example, and particularly when you're hunting with an outfitter or working out of some type of big-game hunting ranch, it's highly likely that butchering facilities will be available to guests. The same is true throughout the deep South, where commercial deer-hunting lodges have flourished in recent years.

Sometimes, hired help at the ranch or lodge tends to all the butchering: you bring in a deer, turn it over to a several-man crew, and they butcher the deer to your specifications, under your watchful eye if you prefer. The individual cuts are then wrapped, labeled as to the type of cut and your name, then placed in a freezer. When you're ready to leave for home, the various packages are then transferred to camping coolers. In many instances such butchering is included in the hunting fee paid, other times it's extra. In any case, tips for the hired help are in order, just as you'd tip your guide and the camp cook.

Other times, a rancher or lodge operator will simply make available a work space where hunters can butcher their deer themselves, which is a good way to kill time while waiting for your partners to fill their tags.

Or perhaps you're not at a commercial operation but hunting with a friend or relative in a distant state and want to full butcher your deer on location to simplify your travel logistics.

It goes without saying that all of these possibilities should be ascertained in advance of your hunting trip, because if you decide to butcher your deer at the hunting site you'll want to have planned ahead and brought along wrapping supplies, tape, knives, and other essentials.

In all of the above cases, however–whether you actually do the butchering yourself or have someone else at the hunting facility do it–you'll leave for home with many frozen packages of venison, which brings up still other concerns.

For those who aren't aware of it, once meat is solidly frozen it should never be allowed to completely defrost and then be refrozen again. This means the hunter will have to evaluate his own particular travel situation and take necessary measures to properly care for his venison through the duration of his journey.

An insulated cooler packed tight with wrapped packages of frozen venison will remain completely frozen for about thirty hours, depending upon the air temperature and the type of container being used. This thirty-hour time frame should be more than sufficient to drive all the way home, where the still-frozen packages can then be transferred to your freezer. But if the driving distance is somewhat longer, or if the air temperature is unseasonably warm, other steps must be taken to preserve the venison.

A hunter's first inclination might be to buy ice along the way and place it in the camping cooler with the frozen venison packages. Don't! The only time ice should be used is for the purpose of keeping unfrozen venison very cold. Otherwise, ice actually has an adverse effect, which involves simple principles of physics. Ice is a liquid (water) that freezes at 32°F.

Meat, however, is a solid commonly frozen at 0°F. It stands to reason, then, that ice, although very cold, is nevertheless warmer than frozen venison and will therefore cause the venison to begin defrosting faster than if no ice is used at all. Consequently, instead of using conventional frozen-water ice, use dry ice, which is frozen and compressed carbon dioxide.

Dry ice is available across the country in all major cities and is most commonly sold by meat markets and stores that specialize in ice cream and dairy products. Upon leaving your hunting location, simply stop at the first large city and check a local phone book's Yellow Pages under the listings "ice" or "refrigeration" for the nearest facility that sells dry ice.

Dry ice, which is carbon dioxide frozen to minus 109°F, remains at this temperature as it gradually dissipates over a period of time. Unlike frozen-water ice, which melts and thereby changes into a liquid, dry ice gradually breaks down by "sublimating," or going from a solid state back to a gas with no formation of liquid. As a result, it is neat, clean, and convenient to use. And since it's capable of freezing meat five times faster than a conventional freezer, it's an unsurpassed method of keeping frozen venison frozen during a long drive home.

To offer an illustration of the mind-boggling capabilities of dry ice, consider this: a four-pound package of unfrozen venison that is sandwiched between two inch-thick slabs of dry ice will be frozen rock solid in only six minutes! As a result, when a similar-size piece of dry ice is placed in the middle of a cooler of already frozen venison packages, they'll stay that way for as long as the ice lasts (until it completely sublimates, in about forty-eight hours at 75°F). When the dry ice disappears, the venison will remain frozen for an additional thirty-six hours, whereupon the ice can be replenished if necessary.

A few words of caution are in order. As the dry ice sublimates, some provision should be made to allow the carbon-dioxide gas to vent; briefly cracking each cooler lid for several seconds at each pit stop is sufficient. Also, never touch or handle dry ice with your bare hands as it is so cold it will actually burn you; use heavy leather gloves, or a thick piece of towel.

By the same token, dry ice should never be allowed to come in direct contact with your wrapped packages of venison or instantaneous freezer burn will result. So be sure to wrap the dry ice in several layers of newspaper before surrounding it in your cooler with the venison packages.

Dry ice is perfect when traveling long distances by vehicle. A four-pound package of unfrozen venison sandwiched between two inch-thick slabs of dry ice will be frozen rock solid in only six minutes!

Other Transportation Methods

When embarking upon that special faraway deer-hunting adventure that requires flying, still other problems present themselves.

Many hunters take one or two modest-size camping coolers, each containing butchering and wrapping supplies, a small duffle bag, and miscellaneous hunting clothing such as boots and outerwear. At the conclusion of the hunt, the trip home sees the clothing go into the duffle bag and the venison packages go into the cooler.

At the airport, the cooler is checked as regular baggage; if you have more than one cooler, you might pay an excess baggage fee. But, more important, make sure the cooler is clearly marked "Rush–Perishable Food." And make sure that, in addition to its latch, the cooler is wrapped with duct tape to prevent the lid from popping open. If the flight home is less than two days, your tightly packed venison will remain solidly frozen. Tell your outfitter to ship your antlers to you by UPS; standard procedure is for him to simply place them in a heavy-duty cardboard box with crumpled newspaper for padding.

When traveling by commercial airlines, primal cuts can be stowed in camping coolers and checked as regular baggage.

Since it is not uncommon these days for flights to be delayed or cancelled, a contingency plan is called for. Most airports have a freezer facility on the grounds for short-term storage of food items and medical supplies and they'll take your cooler(s) at little or no charge. If it's a small airport that doesn't have such a freezer, and you have stay overnight at a local hotel to wait for a flight the following day, make your hotel selection based upon which one will store your cooler; most large hotels that have restaurants have a large walk-in freezer and are usually glad to accommodate their guests.

In still other cases, it may be prudent to have a local processor butcher, wrap, and ship your venison to you. This is displeasing to most hunters who prefer to do all the butchering themselves, which is what this book is all about. But upon rare occasion the travel logistics of an outing do not allow for it and the only alternative is to leave the venison behind, which is even more disagreeable.

When an outfitter ships venison to a hunter-client, the customary procedure is for the venison packages to be solidly frozen and tightly packed in a heavy-duty plastic-coated cardboard container, sometimes with dry ice but usually not. The container (s) are then shipped one or two days after the hunter has left for home, sent by air-freight express so they'll arrive in his hometown within twenty-four hours; the cost averages seventy-five dollars per one hundred pounds of total container weight, and the airport will call you to pick up your venison as soon as it arrives.

7

Home Care of Deer and Aging Your Venison

E ven five hundred years ago, when Native Americans controlled most of the continent and European pioneers were just getting established, no garden crop, catch of fish, or successful trapline-run drew as much celebration as a hunter returning home with a winter's supply of venison. So as you enter your driveway, successful hunter returning home with venison in tow, savor your accomplishment, for you've just completed a hunting ritual that is as old as time.

But don't dawdle with your thoughts too long, for there are important chores to attend to that will weigh heavily upon the quality of the venison you'll regularly be feeding your family. It's important to emphasize this because too often we attribute the quality of a wild game meal to the recipe chosen or the cooking method used. In reality, the quality and condition of the main ingredient given the chef is what determines his or her success.

When confronted with a sight like this, hunters reenact a ritual that is as old as time. But once you arrive back home with your trophy, don't dawdle. There's plenty of important work to be done.

Essentially, what the hunter has to do now is hang his deer, remove the hide, clean the carcass again, and otherwise prepare it for butchering operations. However, the exact sequence in which these tasks are done is far from cut and dried because many variables, including the unique circumstances of any specific hunt, enter the picture. For example, the deer may already be minus its coat, this particular step having been taken care of in camp. Perhaps the deer is even partially butchered and is in the form of primal cuts that are in iced-down coolers. Then too, the existing air temperature will play a role in determining which tasks should be given priority.

Therefore, the only way for me to handle the presentation of material in this chapter is by taking a shotgun approach. In other words, I cover all pertinent techniques and advice regarding the home care of venison. But then it's up to you to perform these procedures in the particular sequence that seems best given the condition of your deer and other variables such as weather.

The only common thread of advice governing all is to proceed at once! Upon arriving home, always attend first to your venison's immediate needs; unpacking clothes, cleaning equipment and putting it away, and catching upon a stack of mail and newspapers can wait.

Hanging Your Deer, Again

If you'll recall, I recommended hanging the deer by the hind legs when it was first brought into camp, for two reasons. First, body heat can more easily rise and escape from the chest region of the animal to more quickly cool the meat; simultaneously, any remaining blood and residual body fluids can quickly drain from the head-neck-thorax region without drippping down and through the prime cuts of venison.

But with your deer already thoroughly chilled, drained of all fluids, and transported home, it can now be rehung in any manner that suits you. I've personally found it much easier to first remove the long backstrap sections, followed by the front legs, then the neck, and finally the rear legs, so I hang the deer by the rear legs. If you prefer to work in some other sequence, fine.

However, one thing you may wish to consider once again is the possibility of having a head mount made by a taxidermist, in which case strangling the deer with a rope

In hanging a deer at home, a convenient tree in the backyard is the most common method. But much better is an enclosed building where you can control all variables; hot or bitter-cold temperatures, inclement weather, roaming neighborhood dogs, and critters such as birds can rob you of your venison.

noose around the neck or antlers is likely to damage the hide.

Other than deciding how to hang the deer, it is equally important to determine where to hang it. Using a stout tree limb in the backyard is a common practice but one I cannot recommend unless no other choice is available. A deer hanging from a tree limb is outside a protected enclosure and may be exposed to inclement weather. Additionally, since the tree's leaves likely are gone, your venison will be subjected to bright sunlight and perhaps even warm temperatures, particularly if you live in the South or took your deer early in the fall while bowhunting. Ideally, the place for hanging your deer should be shaded, a bit breezy, and protected from neighborhood pets roaming at large. Consequently, a garage or shed with a door is perfect, but even an open-air shed or carport may work fine if your neighbors' dogs and cats don't run free.

Hoist the deer so its head, or hind legs, are approximately two feet off the ground. It's virtually impossible for one person to do this alone as overhead beams and roof joists are squared off along their dimensions and a rope defies being pulled over such acute edges.

That's why a hunter should buy a lightweight block and tackle utilizing one or more opposing pulleys. Sportsmen's models, specifically intended for lifting big-game animals, are inexpensive and allow one person to easily winch his deer aloft, either in camp or at home. As an alternative, many hunters who hang their deer in the same place at home, year after year, rig some type of permanent overhead pulley fitted with a rope and gambrel so it's always ready and waiting.

On the subject of using a gambrel, exercise extreme care in slitting the thin skin of the hocks, through which the gambrel is to be inserted, because if you inadvertently cut the Achilles tendon, that particular leg will flop free and be useless for hanging the deer. The only alternative then is to hang the deer by the head.

Aging Venison

The reasons for aging venison are manyfold. Of course, there's the gratifying opportunity of being able to admire the game a while longer. But from a strict meat-care standpoint, aging imparts tenderness and enhances the venison's flavor by allowing the slow, controlled growth of natural bacterial organisms to break down tissue cells. Once a deer has been properly aged, butchering and quick freezing then brings an immediate halt to any further bacterial action, which preserves the meat.

The act of aging venison carries an almost romantic quality, but some hunters go to extremes and age their deer far longer than necessary. This is risky business because if you go beyond the point of merely tenderizing the

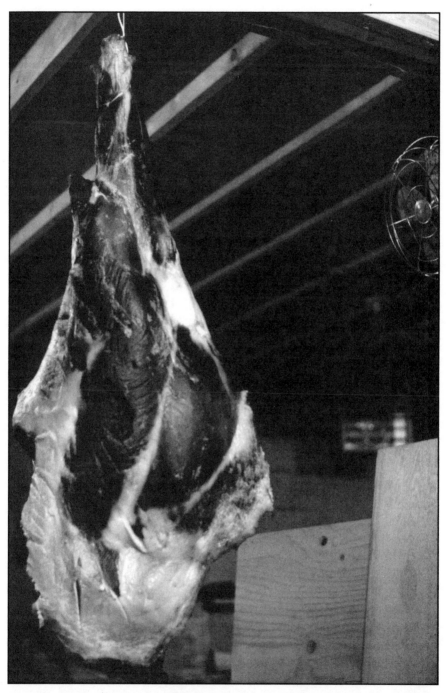

Properly aging venison means subjecting it to the proper temperature and humidity for a prescribed length of time to tenderize the meat. The animal can be aged whole, or if outside conditions prevent this, primal cuts can be aged in a basement or even your refrigerator. (photo by Kenn Oberrecht)

meat there's the possibility spoilage may begin to set in.

Perfect aging is accomplished under these conditions: the deer should be hanging, with its hide on, for a length of time ranging from four to eight days, at a temperature consistently between 38° and 40°F, at a relative humidity of seventy-five to eighty percent.

However, this is the ideal, and it is not often that these conditions can be met exactly. Take the matter of air temperature. If the mercury climbs to 50° or 60°F during the day, but then dips down into the twenties at night, no problem; the temperature of the meat itself will still remain in the desirable 38° to 40°F range. Just remember never to allow the meat to freeze while aging; nor should the temperature of the meat ever climb above 45°F or bacterial growth will be accelerated. One way to monitor the temperature of your aging carcass is to use an ice pick to pierce a hole into the neck meat and insert a thermometer.

As to the recommended length of time venison should be allowed to age, again a bit of flexibility is permissible. Although the ideal time is four to eight days, ten days will do no harm if optimum air temperatures prevail. Similarly, if the deer you take is in prime condition, as described in Chapter 1, you may commence butchering operations after only one or two day's hanging time with the full assurance that the venison will be tender and flavorful.

Regarding aging time, another important point to keep in mind is that the clock begins ticking the moment the animal expires. So if your deer hung in camp for three days, and then it was a two-day drive home, your venison has already aged five days before even arriving at your intended butchering location.

The best way to monitor the humidity is by simply listening to a daily weather report, which most hunters do anyway in camp with a portable weather radio. A relatively high humidity index, around seventy percent or so, is desired to ensure moisture retention by the meat.

Venison, which is already quite dry and lean, may actually become less tender if the humidity is exceedingly low. This is why it's always recommended that hunters living in the desert Southwest and far North not age their game any longer than the brief period it hangs in camp; in such consistently dry areas of the continent, aging actually has an adverse effect.

Conversely, if the humidity is consistently too high–eighty-five percent or higher–which often is characteristic of the southeastern states and lower Midwest, the added moisture in the air not only spurs bacteria growth but may also encourage the formation of mold on the outside of the meat. Once again, a deer taken in these regions should not be aged longer than the brief time it hangs in camp.

Under favorable temperature and humidity conditions, a deer should ideally age with the hide on because it helps the carcass to retain moisture.

This not only prevents it from drying out too much but also eliminates excessive surface-skin hardening or glazing that must later be trimmed away, at the sacrifice of a good deal of prime meat. However, if the hide has already been removed in camp, due to overly warm weather or the need to reduce the carcass to primal cuts for transportation purposes, there is no alternative but to age the meat without its overcoat. To offer a bit of protection, slip a gamebag over the animal or enclose the primal cuts in separate, smaller bags.

In momentarily going back to the subject of hanging a deer, there's a third hanging method most hunters are unaware of that some of the most accomplished chefs make use of. Quite different from hanging a deer by the hind legs, or by the head, this method involves hanging the deer by a single hook or rope that is passed through the bony channel through the pelvis just beneath the Aitch bone, which formerly housed the bladder.

The technique is called the tender-stretch hanging method and it's specifically designed for those deer a hunter may suspect are not likely to be tender; you know, the eight year-old Boone & Crockett buck you couldn't resist shooting because of his huge rack, despite the fact that his coat was ragged and thin, his muzzle was gray, and he limped along with arthritis.

Compared to hanging a deer by the head or hind legs, both of which see the brunt of the carcass weight borne by the hanging device, tender-stretch hanging strains and pushes the weight of the meat against itself to good advantage. That is, when the deer is hanging by the pelvic arch, the heavy weight of the unsupported hindquarters is allowed to exert downward pressure upon the remainder of the carcass. This has the effect of stretching the longitudinal muscle fibers (which are always the toughest) and thereby somewhat breaking down the integrity of their cellular structure, which in turn makes them more tender.

To gain maximum advantage from this technique, two other steps are necessary. First, in addition to hanging the deer by the pelvic arch, tie a concrete block to a short length of rope tied around the neck (or to the antlers), which further pulls and stretches downward upon the carcass to make the neck meat and upper regions of the front shoulders tender beyond belief. Then, after a couple of days of hanging and aging, turn the deer around so it is now hanging by the head, with the concrete block tied between the knees of both rear legs; a three-foot length of pipe through the gambrel slits, to which the rope is tied, works fine. This stretches the deer in the opposite direction and tenderizes both hindquarters and the saddle.

To repeat, in most cases the tender-stretch procedure is not necessary. Rather, it's a refinement of traditional aging, designed to tenderize those occasional animals that upon close inspection appear not to be as tender as desired, but which the hunter doesn't want to relegate entirely to the meat grinder.

There are still other aspects of aging that warrant careful thought. If it is terribly hot outside, and even a brief aging period might cause spoilage, I recommend stripping the hide off your deer if you haven't already done so and immediately butchering the animal. Wrap all the meat cuts, but instead of placing them in your freezer, place them in your refrigerator.

The inside of your refrigerator has an average temperature of 38°F, which will allow for a week of perfect aging. One important thing to understand, however, is that the inside of your refrigerator has a very low humidity level, which will cause your venison to become overly dry as it ages if special precautions are not taken. To add moisture to the air, set an uncovered bowl of water inside the refrigerator; or, soak a thick bath towel, partially wring it out, and set it on a middle rack of the fridge.

It might seem that all of the wrapped venison packages from a recently butchered deer, when placed in a standard-size refrigerator, would leave no room for the family's wide assortment of other food items. Yet keep in mind that only the prime cuts, the steaks and roasts, benefit from any aging procedure. The significant quantity of scraps and trimmings that will shortly go into the production of burger and sausage do not benefit from aging, as the meat-grinder's blades will "tenderize" those venison parts. These wrapped packages can go straight from the butchering table into the freezer.

Likewise, the liver and heart, if they weren't already eaten in camp and are to be saved for future use, don't benefit from aging and they, too, can immediately go into the freezer.

The same is true of those large, irregularly shaped meat chunks from the neck, brisket, lower legs, or elsewhere that eventually will find themselves cut into small chunks and transformed into soups and stews. They will become tenderized during the long, slow-simmering, moist-heat cooking methods traditionally used in recipes for these cuts.

If, despite all of this, there still is not enough room in the refrigerator for the family's usual array of foods plus one's wrapped venison packages, simply haul out your camping coolers. Ice them down to keep milk, eggs, and whatnot cold for a few days; it's a minor inconvenience that most families who relish prime, aged venison are fully willing to put up with.

Now let's look at conditions that are just the opposite. Suppose that instead of being overly warm outside, it's bitter cold and a deer allowed to hang outside will quickly freeze solid. The easiest solution, if you have a garage, small shed, or similar storage building, is to close all the doors and windows and turn on a small electric space heater in a far corner. It won't be terribly expensive to operate for a few days because, remember, you only have to maintain a 38°F temperature.

Another alternative, if you don't have an outside storage building but do have a basement, is to hang the venison in the form of primal cuts (front and back legs, saddle, etc.) from ceiling joists via short lengths of rope. Some hunters do this in a far corner, where there is a window they can crack open, and then fashion a "stall" from a tarp that surrounds the hanging venison and prevents the rest of the basement from becoming too cold.

Removing the Hide

I've mentioned the subject of skinning deer several times, and this is a good place to examine the subject in detail. The hunter himself, however, will have to decide exactly when to remove the deer's hide, depending upon a wide range of factors such as the existing temperature and weather conditions, how the deer is to be transported home, and in what manner the deer is to be aged. All of this presents something of a dilemma.

If you can skin the deer immediately after it is killed, or within a few hours, while the hide is still fresh and warm, it will peel off quickly and easily, especially when compared to the tough work involved in trying to wrench it off days later when it is cold and much drier. But, as already noted, leaving the hide on, if the weather permits, is beneficial because it protects the carcass during transport and helps the venison retain moisture during aging. What to do?

Well, only you can answer that. My opinion regarding any decision about deer care is that the quality of the venison should always be given priority. I have trained myself to tolerate the more difficult work that delayed hide removal entails, knowing the venison will be all the better.

Begin by hanging the deer by either the head or hind legs, whichever you prefer. It makes no difference.

Next, slit the skin on the inside of each leg, just above the knee, being sure to make the cut very shallow so as to not damage any meat, and continue those slits to where the legs join the body's main trunk area.

Assuming you're not planning to have a head mount made, next make a cut through the hide encircling the neck, just below the chin.

Now, extend the abdominal cut you made when field dressing by going right down the centerline of the chest, brisket, and neck to the neck cut you just completed.

In making all of these cuts, use just the tip of your knife with the blade edge facing up. The same knife you use for field dressing is adequate for this chore.

Now reach for your skinning knife, the one with the wide, flat blade designed to be worked beneath animal hides without damaging meat. Grab a flap of the hide at the neck and begin pulling it down and away with your hand, using the knife to help free the hide wherever it is securely attached. Or, if the deer is hanging by the legs, free the hide from around the legs first, being careful not to cut through the Achilles tendons, then around the tail.

The remainder of the hide-removal procedure is accomplished mostly with the hands alone. Grab the hide, roll it just a bit to get a secure hand-

In removing the hide, use your knife minimally to avoid cutting into the venison directly beneath. Much of the hide can be pulled off by merely rolling it into a cylinder and removing it off by hand, much like peeling a banana.

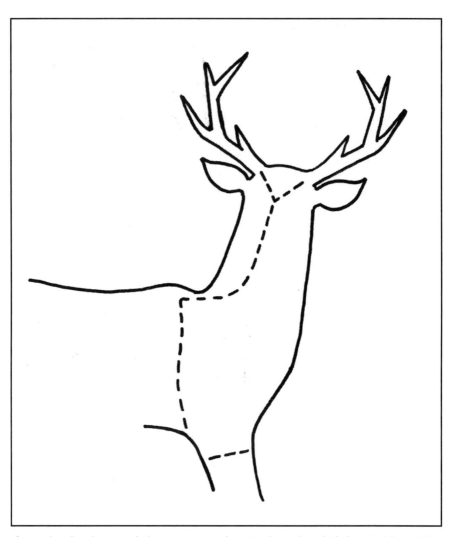

If your deer head is intended to go to a taxidermist, don't short-hide his work by cutting the head off at the neck. Give him plenty of cape to work with by cutting behind the front shoulder. Never cut the skin in the front, throat region; instead, cut up the centerline of the back of the neck.

hold, and then, with the weight of your body, begin pushing downward with your fists. As the hide begins to come away from the carcass it can be rolled even more for a firmer grasp and therefore additional leverage. The advantage of this method is that it eliminates the chance of accidental slices into the meat or hide that even an expert might make if he used a knife continually.

After removing the hide, you may wish to saw off each lower hind leg just below the knees, especially if you plan to enclose the carcass in a game-bag. Otherwise, the lower legs may be removed later during the initial butchering operations.

It's now a good idea to inspect the carcass for damaged or bloodshot areas that should be trimmed away. Pay particular attention to the region of the gunshot or arrow wound. If a shoulder or any other part of the deer has been damaged by the bullet or arrow, it may be salvageable. Simply place the meat overnight in a bowl of salt water. Nine times in ten bloodshot meat looks worse than it really is, and this overnight soaking does an impressive job of cleaning it up and restoring it to an acceptable state for use in burger or sausage. If the bloodshot area is too severe, or appears riddled with digestive matter or pieces of splintered bone, discard it.

Next, use a clean cloth dampened with warm water to wipe down the exterior of your deer carcass. As careful as anyone may try to be in skinning a deer, it is inevitable that hairs from the hide will be found clinging to the carcass and a warm, dampened cloth is the fastest way to remove them.

Finally, we should say a few words about taxidermy. Although this subject is worthy of an entire book in itself, there are a few important points that should be made here because they directly relate to the differing way in which the hide should be removed.

First, the hide should be removed at the earliest opportunity when it is still "green" and easily pulls away. After the hide has set—begun to dry and tightly adhere to the carcass—less hand pulling and far more knife cutting is required to remove it. This greatly increases the chance of an errant slice damaging the skin.

Another common error many hunters make is not removing enough hide and simply cutting the head off in the vicinity of the neck region. Taxidermists wince at this because it gives the finished head an inferior amputated look.

The most admirable head mounts reveal not only the entire neck region of the animal but also the brisket and beginning contours of the front shoulders and back, giving the trophy much greater presence and dimension.

So when removing the hide, always cut well behind the front shoulders as you encircle the chest region with your knife cut.

Next, from the sternum, carefully make a cut just to the beginning of the insides of the forelegs, with subsequent cuts going down the insides of the legs to the knees. Never continue the brisket cut up the entire length of the front of the neck because this part of the deer is clearly on display and difficult to mend.

With these cuts made, now make another cut down the centerline of the back of the neck to the base of the skull, with additional cuts then going to the base of each antler as shown in the accompanying diagram. On the finished mount these cuts, which later will be sewn together by the taxidermist, will be out of sight. Now carefully begin peeling the hide down and away from the shoulder/neck region, using your knife blade as little as possible. The goal is to expose the entire neck so that the meat may be salvaged, but at this stage it is not necessary to actually remove the meat from the carcass; it can be left intact with the remainder of the deer.

As the hide is gradually removed around the outside of the neck and up to the chin area, go no farther. Simply cut through the neck bone so the head will fall free with its attached cape intact. Your taxidermist will undoubtedly prefer to attend to the remainder of delicate skinning around the eyes, mouth, and other head parts.

Finally, liberally apply salt to the inside of the cape, including as far as possible up into the throat region and inside the nostrils and mouth. The head with its attached cape can now be secured inside a heavy-duty plastic garbage bag and transported to your taxidermist; or, the works can go into a large chest freezer for a month or more.

8

Preparing to Butcher
Your Deer

In getting ready for butchering, the hunter will need to assemble a
selection of tools that will enable him to reduce big pieces of venison
quickly and efficiently into many smaller ones ready for the freezer. In
accomplishing this, first-hand, trial-and-error experience plays a role
in determining what works best for you. And those special routines,
methods, and equipment preferences you eventually come to rely upon year-
in and year-out are sure to differ somewhat from those of another hunter
who is equally proficient in handling his deer.

Then there is an entirely different class of hunters–the professionals–whom
we should all watch and talk to whenever the opportunity arises.

One such "professor emeritus" of the chopping-block table who long
ago took me under his wing is Minnesota hunter Charlie Hause. Aside from

When conditions
are right and
everyone in
camp is filling
his tag, a meat-
cutting marathon
may be in your
future. To make
the job easy, first
spend some time
assembling your
tools and
preparing your
work area.

being a fanatical deer hunter, he's a professional meatcutter by trade. In addition to annually cutting up hundreds of carcasses from beef steers and hogs, and the deer he harvests himself, he moonlights during the hunting season by doing custom-butchering for local sportsmen.

I don't know how many deer Charlie has cut up over the years, but there was a particular day that stands out in his memory, a day when he was so swamped with orders he just couldn't handle everything himself. So he bought a couple of cases of premium beer, which is always a good persuader, and then called three fellow meatcutters to help him out of a jam. Beginning at three o'clock in the afternoon, the foursome set to the task and continued working through the late night hours until four o'clock in the morning. During that time Charlie and his pals completely butchered a total of forty deer. Not only that, they also made 1,200 pounds of burger and sausage from all the lesser cuts and trimmings, swapped stories of hunts past and, yes, even managed to polish off both cases of beer.

It must have been a wild and woolly night, but everything was completed to perfection and many hours later hundreds of wrapped, labeled, and frozen packages of venison were waiting for their respective owners to pick up. I remember Charlie saying that about the time he finished cleaning up his home butchershop from this marathon meatcutting session, he had just enough time to shower and gulp down several cups of black coffee before having to open his meat market downtown. A pro's pro, indeed!

Getting Your Work Area Ready

Even though professional butchers have personal preferences when it comes to certain brands of cutting tools and supplies, their common bond is that, before setting to the task at hand, they invest a lot of time readying their work sites.

This is critical to success, speed, and happiness because you don't want to be so physically uncomfortable that the butchering operation becomes a miserable ordeal. Nor do you want it to take twelve hours to complete a six-hour task, and perhaps even do a sloppy job at that. And with several venison quarters lying before you, now is certainly not the time to launch a search for your knives, try to locate your whetstone, or find you have to go to town to buy freezer wrapping paper and other supplies; this is nothing more than poor planning, and it often dooms what should be a proficient butchering effort right from the get-go.

First decide upon the best place to do your butchering. Since everyone's living circumstances are different, I'll simply describe the best and worst places and the reader can adjust this insight to his own situation.

The best location is a clean, well-lit, spacious garage that is cool enough for meat handling but warm enough that you can work in shirtsleeves.

The least favorable location is your kitchen, and with good reason. The kitchens of most homes are high-traffic areas where meals must be prepared several times a day and hunting dogs must be fed and kids are always looking for snacks or wanting a drink. Also, most kitchens are too warm for long meatcutting sessions, and available table or counter-top workspace isn't really large enough for major butchering operations.

What you need is ample time and space to complete your meatcutting without hassles and interruptions. You need a large work surface and plenty of elbow room, particularly if someone else will be working alongside you. And you need the peace of mind, not the constant worry and concern, that some errant speck of blood or scrap of meat that falls to the floor is not going to draw the wrath of other family members.

A large table is fine as your work surface. This is most commonly a picnic table brought inside, but it can be a simple four-by-eight sheet of plywood resting upon sawhorses. Just make sure it's as clean as possible and situated in such a manner that you will be cutting at comfortable waist level.

To ensure cleanliness, cover your work surface with protective paper. Lay it down in several long, overlapping sheets with the shiny, plastic-coated side up; secure the edges in place around the perimeter of the table with masking tape.

The purpose of this tabletop covering is to have a neat, clean place to set various cuts of meat before and after working on them. However, you won't want to do actual cutting on this surface because your knife blade would quickly reduce the paper to shreds.

For cutting work, you need some type of cutting board. This can be a standard kitchen model, if it's extra-large in size, that's made of strips of laminated hardwood and intended for food-preparation work.

Better still is a professional meatcutting board made of pressed styrene and thermoplastic resin that is both sanitary and impervious to knife cuts. In either case, the ideal size is something about twenty-four inches wide by thirty-six inches long by one-inch thick.

Avoid the commonly seen use of a square of plywood. The soft wood

A large, flat cutting surface, such as a chopping block table is essential to meat cutting. Wooden cutting surfaces are porous, however, and require regular cleaning. A one to four-inch thick block of hard plastic is easier to clean than wood and requires less maintenance.

will become scarred with deep knife cuts that attract bacteria, and the wood laminations are glued with chemical adhesives that may be toxic.

Instead of a cutting board that's placed upon the larger work surface, the hunter might want to consider a stand-alone chopping-block table. They're worthwhile investments on the part of serious sportsmen who take several deer every year because, in addition to accommodating venison, they have numerous other fish and game-dressing uses throughout the year.

Just be sure to carefully follow the manufacturer's instructions before and after each use of the table, because even the hardest wood must periodically be cleaned and maintained. The chopping-block table I'm presently using is made of hard-rock maple impregnated with a special food-safe polyurethane coating that requires no maintenance whatever, other than occasionally wiping it down with a rag dampened in very hot water. Most, however, require periodic scraping with a stiff-bristle wire brush and then a soaking-application with disinfectant followed by a treatment with a bactericidal mineral oil.

Cutting Tools that Get the Job Done

"A meatcutter is no better than the knives he uses," Jim Borg, a professional butcher from Nashville, Tennessee, remarked as we began working on two deer. With that, he opened his special briefcase, a hallmark that distinguishes such tradesmen, and gave me a peek at a gleaming array of knives of every conceivable design, all assigned to their own protective slots in plastic foam.

Borg's opening comment was right on target because, like a master mechanic given only one size and type of wrench, a hunter who has only one poorly chosen knife can expect to do little more than an amateurish, hacked-up job on his deer.

Since every skilled meatcutter eventually acquires preferences in his chosen assortment of cutting tools, it's impossible here to recommend a specific selection of knives as better than any other. Yet, we can talk in generalities.

First, some type of conventional butcher's knife with a blade at least ten inches in length is needed to reduce large chunks of meat to smaller ones in one fell swoop; otherwise, with a shorter blade, several smaller cuts will have to be made instead of a single slice, and those cuts will seldom meet, leaving a ragged, irregular appearance.

A boning knife also is imperative. As the reader will soon discover, I'm a strong proponent of boning-out meat whenever possible, for two important reasons. Bone-cutting with a saw is eliminated, so marrow "dust" cannot sprinkle the meat; many butchers believe marrow, in addition to deer fat, is what's often responsible for the overly strong, pungent, gamey flavor that many people object to. Second, you save on freezer space if you don't have to store forty pounds of bones (which you cannot eat, anyway) along with your venison.

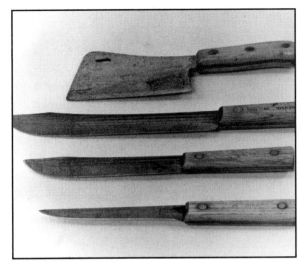

An assemblage of knives is important, each intended for a specific task. The author recommends (from top to bottom) a cleaver, a long- and short-bladed butcher's knife, and a boning knife. Also needed is an all-purpose utility knife, not shown because your choice of hunting/field-dressing knife is adequate.

Most boning knives have a long, slender blade that culminates in an upswept tip. They are also quite thin, which gives the blade flexibility to allow a cutter to guide the blade around irregular bone curvatures. And guess what? One way a sportsman can make at least one of his knives perform double-duty is to use his long-bladed fish-fillet knife as his venison boning knife; it's a near-perfect substitute.

An all-purpose or utility knife, or even a paring knife, will also come in handy for final trimming operations and other close work calling for a meticulous touch. And from time to time you might also find use for a heavy meat cleaver, especially when working on ribs and steaks prepared bone-in.

Some type of meat saw is also sure to be periodically needed in the processing of venison. As already mentioned, I'm a proponent of minimal bone cutting, but since some cutting is inevitable, a quality saw is a delight to work with. Such a saw is chiefly used to cut off the lower legs and separate the head from the carcass by cutting through the neckbone. Then, during actual butchering operations, you may desire to cut sections from the rib cage for broiling, and certain types of roasts, such as front-shoulder blade roasts. There's even one preliminary butchering technique to be described later that involves first halving the carcass by cutting down the centerline of the backbone. There are many models of meat saws to choose from, depending upon your needs and how much you can afford to spend. The smallest I'm aware of is the Wyoming Saw, available through hunting mail-order catalogs and designed primarily for field use or in camp.

The largest and most expensive saw is an electric, table-mounted bandsaw of the type found in professional butchershops. Although they do extremely high-quality work in short time, their prices generally limit their use to those who do custom-butchering of deer for others, and hunting clubs where many members can share both the saw and its cost.

In between these two extremes are moderately priced, professional meat saws that resemble giant hacksaws but are specifically intended for cutting meat and bone.

Do yourself a favor and don't cheap-out by attempting to use a conventional hacksaw from your garage workshop. Hacksaws, generally used for metal cutting, typically have twenty to twenty-six teeth per inch; since the teeth are so small and close together they quickly clog with bone and meat residue, which renders them inoperative until they're scrubbed down with a stiff-bristle brush. You don't need this continual hassle. Buy a professional meat saw, which has only ten to twelve teeth per inch. It will be a pleasure to use, will last the rest of your life (you'll probably never even have to replace the blade), and the only maintenance you'll have to give it is to wash it with hot, soapy water at the end of each day's use.

A professional meat saw can make short work of many deer, but they are pricey, which usually limits them to hunting clubs where many members can share the cost.

A traditional butcher's meat saw is a smart investment for any serious hunter. Though not cheap, such a saw will last a lifetime.

Some means of keeping your knives scalpel-sharp through the duration of your meatcutting also is imperative. A quality whetstone such as an Arkansas or Ouachita is a good choice, and so are the ceramic rods and diamond-dust-impregnated steel rods now available to hunters.

It would be impossible to describe a universal knife-sharpening procedure here, because so many variables are involved, including the type of steel the blade is made of, the shape of the blade, whether the blade is flat- or hollow-ground, and whether the bevel of the cutting edge is straight or chiseled. Good advice is to follow the sharpening instructions in the booklet that came with each specific knife; you did save them, didn't you?

Once a knife is sharp, most expert meatcutters make periodic use of a sharpening steel. A steel looks like a large rat-tail file in that a long, tapered, rough-surfaced rod is inserted into a wooden or hard-plastic handle.

The purpose of a steel is not to actually sharpen a knife in the conventional sense, by removing metal and forming an edge, as with a stone. Rather, in the midst of cutting chores, a steel allows the user to quickly but temporarily restore

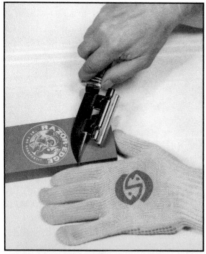

Some means of keeping your knives sharp is essential. Since blade designs widely differ, study the instructions that came with your specific brand for the manufacturer's recommendations.

A butcher's steel is both inexpensive and a fast and easy way to keep knives sharp between sessions at the sharpening stone.

the blade's sharpness by removing the wavy edge all knives take after use; with the microscopic edge of teeth periodically once again made straight and "true," the worker can delay actual stone-sharpening for lengthy periods of time.

At first, using a steel may seem somewhat awkward, but with some practice it will quickly be just like second nature. Basically, the knife is held in one hand, tip pointing up, and the steel is held in the other, tip pointing up. The knife is then gently sandpapered against the steel in rapid up and down fashion, with each pass seeing the knife alternate across the front of the steel and then the back, to work both sides of the blade. If you find any difficulty performing this maneuver, ask a butcher at a meat market to give you a firsthand demonstration.

Tricks of the Trade

Among the little tips and techniques you can pick up by watching other experts is one that Charlie Hause passed onto me many years ago, and that is making sure that the meat is very, very cold. The shoulders, haunches, and other primal cuts should be almost but not quite frozen. The reason for this is that when it is warm, any kind of meat is loose, floppy, soft, and uncontrollable, and in this condition it's virtually impossible to make neat, precision cuts.

Furthermore, a large quantity of relatively warm meat from any kind of animal, domestic or wild, has a distinct odor. It is not at all an unpleasant aroma, but after six or eight hours of continually breathing it in you may begin feeling a bit nauseous.

Very cold meat, on the other hand, has almost no odor whatsoever. And since it is so firm, you can handle it with ease, propping it up just so to make certain cuts, turning it this way or that to perform all manner of surgical operations cleanly and neatly without the meat sagging, separating, and seemingly having a mind of its own.

Another characteristic of very cold meat is that it is not sticky, which is something no one can really appreciate until he's had the experience of working with warm meat, particularly small pieces being trimmed for burger. Like flypaper, the stuff sticks to your hands, your work surface, your knife blade, and everything else it touches, which generates so much frustration that you want to shoot the deer a second time.

So make a point of ensuring that your venison is quite cold, even if it means putting a large primal cut on a tray and briefly slipping it into your freezer to firm-up while you take a coffee break.

Another thing Charlie Hause emphasizes is the importance of working with clean meat. It is inevitable when working with deer that countless, tiny hairs from the hide will adhere to the venison. These are all sources of contamination if not removed, but picking them away one by one can test even the most patient.

That's why Charlie thoroughly cleans all surfaces of the meat before the first knife cut is made. He does this by using a small piece of terrycloth towel soaked in very warm water and then thoroughly wrung out. Amazingly, several swipes in one direction and then another removes every stray hair easily and quickly. Although this step is also done just before hanging the carcass and letting it age, it's necessary to do it a second time when each primal cut is removed from the carcass and set upon the meatcutting table to be worked upon.

Still another tip—this one from Jim Borg—has to do with testing the tenderness of various meat cuts. Merely pinch a small piece of each major meat cut between the fingernails of your thumb and forefinger. Meat that is not so tender will offer resistance at first and then, upon exertion of more fingertip pressure, will begin to slightly dimple or compress itself. Conversely, tender meat will readily be cut by your fingernails and begins to signal that it's about to "mush" if still more pressure is exerted.

There are several advantages in knowing how tender various parts of the anatomy of that particular deer are likely to be. First, you know how the meat should be cut. Should it be sliced into steaks to be broiled, made into roasts to be baked, or cut into cubes for stew meat? In producing roasts and such, you know whether you should go to the extra trouble to lard or bard particular ones (both of these techniques are discussed later). You even know

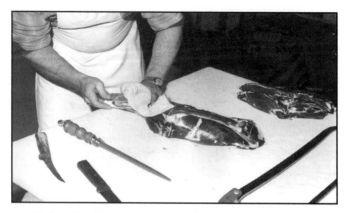

Just before butchering, a neat trick for quickly removing the countless little hairs that cling to deer meat is to wipe the venison down with a damp, hot towel.

whether certain cuts should be tenderized more just before cooking by applying a commercial meat-tenderizing salt or soaking them in some type of marinade.

9

Butchering the Front Legs

utchering a deer is easy if you look at it from this standpoint: the basic thing you'll be doing is using a modest assortment of tools to reduce big pieces of meat into little pieces. It's not exactly rocket science. The somewhat difficult hurdle many hunters must confront is psychological, in that they feel overwhelmed by the enormous size of that deer carcass hanging in the garage and simply don't know where to begin. Several weeks ago, before the deer season opened, they bagged two rabbits and in a matter of minutes after arriving home had them in the frying pan. But now, the antlered beast hanging before them is intimidating.

It needn't be that way, because butchering is not unlike changing a flat tire in that once you've learned which steps have to be performed and then acquire some practice, you can do a professional job almost blindfolded.

My recommendation has always been to approach the hanging carcass piecemeal. In other words, remove one piece of meat that is relatively easy to handle, such as a front leg, take it to the cutting table and, following the step-by-step instructions I'll give in a moment, thoroughly reduce that leg to wrapped cuts of meat ready for the freezer.

Don't allow that huge hanging deer carcass to intimidate you. Divide and conquer by simply tackling the job piecemeal. Let's begin with a front leg.

Then go back to the carcass and get the other front leg and proceed as before, momentarily forgetting about all the rest. Since you've just finished a front leg and learned something in the process about its unique anatomical features, the second front leg should be a snap. Then butcher a hind leg, as described in the next chapter, and so on. By following this suggested routine, the carcass will steadily become smaller and smaller while, conversely, your confidence level will grow and greatly reduce that seemingly formidable challenge you initially faced.

Keep in mind a key thought expressed in the last chapter. You need not follow any specific butchering sequence, such as the front legs before hind legs, or whatever. Feel entirely free to tackle any of the meat-cutting procedures in this book in any order you like.

Moreover, don't worry about making mistakes! Sure, you'll occasionally goof, but will life as we know it on this planet come to a screeching halt? Of course not. And besides, you're going to need to accumulate a hefty pile of scraps and trimmings to produce all the burger and sausage your family is looking forward to.

Some Words About Fat

Before we begin cutting meat it's important to briefly discuss the trimming away of fat we'll be encountering in various places of the deer's anatomy as we go along.

Previous books and magazine articles dealing with the handling of venison have preached the dire necessity of trimming away every speck of fat you find, claiming it is so distasteful that if left intact no one will enjoy eating your venison. This information is not entirely accurate.

Actually, deer possess three types of fat, and according to studies at Utah State University, not all of them are sources of disagreeable or so-called gamey flavor. There is cod fat, which is found only on the brisket (lower-front chest region). There is tallow fat, which is found mainly on the back, covering the rump, and to a lesser extent around the perimeter of the neck and on the rearmost areas of the front shoulders. And there is marbling fat, which is found throughout the body but concentrated in muscle tissue and between series of opposing muscle groups.

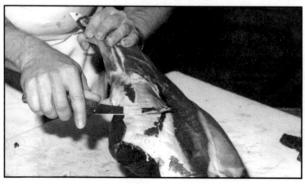

Deer possess several types of fat (tallow, cod, and marbling), but only the tallow, found on the surface, should be removed. A boning or fish-fillet knife makes the job easy.

Cod fat and tallow fat are both designed to help keep the animal warm in cold weather, so nature has located them on the exterior surfaces of the anatomy just beneath the hide. Cod fat and tallow fat have flavors not terribly disagreeable but indeed noticeable and upon occasion a bit strong, particularly in mature animals (those which are three and one-half years of age or older). Good advice is to try and remove as much cod fat and tallow fat as possible. But there's no need to freak out and be so meticulous about this that you end up spending twice the amount of time it should ordinarily take to butcher a deer.

Marbling fat, on the other hand, is deep fat woven interstitially through and between the muscle fibers. It looks like thin, elongated, white streaks, and as much of this fat as possible should be allowed to remain! Not only is marbling fat virtually tasteless, but the research at Utah State proved its presence significantly increases the tenderness of cooked venison compared to other cuts of meat that had much of their marbling removed. As a result, since deer are very active animals possessing very lean meat compared to sedentary animals such as beef steers, it is important to not remove what little marbling the critters possess.

Consequently, when you first lay each large chunk of venison on the cutting table, no matter what part of the anatomy it came from, turn the meat this way and that and, as you do so, carefully trim away as much surface fat as you can see on all sides of the meat. However, after this is accomplished and as you begin to reduce the meat to various freezer-ready cuts, leave intact the remaining fat found deeper inside.

Let's Cut Meat

Removing a front leg/shoulder assembly from the carcass is easy because there is no ball-and-socket attachment as there is with the hind legs. Instead, the wide, flat shoulder bone, which is essentially the size and shape of a ping-pong paddle and is known as the scapula, is free-floating and independent of any other bone connection with the body. It's attached to the body only by several thin muscle segments covered by thin skin and is easily cut with a knife.

At the meatpole, all that's necessary is to grab the leg in the knee region and pull it away from the carcass a bit while simultaneously using a long-bladed butcher knife to cut the connective muscle tissue on the backside of the scapula adjoining the rib cage. Keep the blade flat and tight against the rib cage as you to continue to lift and pull away the shoulder and cut it free. In this manner, you should be able to remove the entire front leg and shoulder assembly in less than one minute.

With the front leg and shoulder now lying on your cutting table, wipe it down with a warm, damp cloth to remove any stray hairs or other debris.

Then, with a thin-bladed knife (a fish fillet knife is fine), begin carefully trimming the meat of unwanted tallow and the very thin, protective, skinlike glazing crust the meat acquired during aging; in many places this procedure will expose pure meat.

There are three meatcutting methods for the front leg and shoulder region, depending upon how you intend to use the meat later on. None of this meat is sinfully tender, so the first and easiest method is to merely cut all of it from the bone, then reduce it into chunks to be used in stews, soups, casseroles, or in the grinding of burger and sausage.

For those who prefer blade and arm roasts (rather than rolled shoulder roasts), simply reduce the front leg to three pieces.

Blade and Arm Roasts

The second method, a bit more time-consuming but not at all difficult, involves laying the leg and shoulder assembly before you with the inside of the leg down and the lower part of the leg facing to the right, in order to produce two bone-in roasts as shown in the accompanying diagram. The first cut removes the lower leg just above the knee; since this lower leg is thoroughly laced with sinew and ligaments, the only value it has, after a good deal of judicious trimming, is fodder for the meat grinder. In creating the two bone-in roasts, the one nearest the lower leg is called an arm roast and the second cut of meat, located beyond this and higher up, is called a blade roast.

When engaging in these two operations, make them neat and professional looking by trying to avoid cutting the meat itself with your saw. Cut down as far as possible through the meat with your

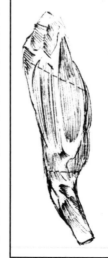

The lowermost leg part, just below the knee, is sinewy and goes into the burger pile to be ground later. Now cut the remaining shoulder in half, approximately through the middle so two roasts of equal weight are created.

knife, using the saw only when you come to bone.

I suggest using this method, in the producing of two shoulder roasts, only if you have an adult buck or doe. Younger deer have front leg-shoulder regions that simply do not possess enough meat to produce arm or shoulder roasts of any significant size that would provide a meal for more than one person.

Rolled Shoulder Roasts

The third meatcutting method, still a bit more time-consuming, involves boning out the meat to produce sumptuous, rolled shoulder roasts. Since the meat from both the arm and blade regions of both legs is combined into one roast, there is, in this case, enough meat even on a smaller, younger animal to produce a single roast that's adequate in size to feed a family of four; if it's a larger, adult animal, the completed roast will be so sizeable it can actually be sliced in half to yield two four-person meals.

To produce a rolled shoulder roast, begin by laying the meat with the inside of the leg down and the lower leg pointing away from you. You'll immediately see a distinct white line vertically separating the right one-third of the shoulder from the left two-thirds. This is actually the top edge of a bony ridge standing upright on one side of the ping-pong-paddle-shaped scapula. Butchers commonly refer to the oblong meat on the right side of the bony ridge as scotch roll meat, and that to the left as the clod meat.

Run your knife blade close to the left side of the vertical bone ridge and down through the clod meat until the knife edge stops on the flat scapula, then turn the blade flat and continue slicing toward the left until you almost reach the edge of that side of the shoulder.

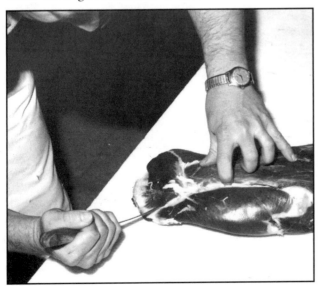

To produce a rolled shoulder roast, the meat needs to be boned-out. Find the vertical-standing bone ridge in the middle of the shoulder and run your knife blade down one side, across the adjacent boney flat and around the edge, being careful not to cut all the way through the meat.

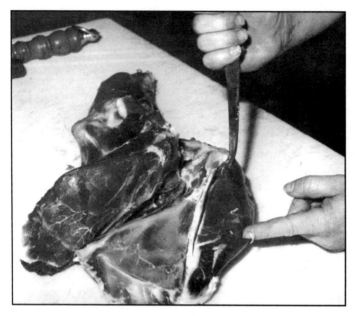

Next run your knife blade down the opposite side of the vertical bone ridge and around to that opposite side.

Now cut down on the right side of the vertical bone ridge through the scotch roll meat until the knife blade stops on that side of the scapula, and continue slicing all the way to the right (a distance of about two inches).

Use just the tip of your knife blade in carrying out these two steps. As you approach the far left and far right edges, be careful not to cut the two pieces of meat free from the bone just yet, because you want to next turn the works over and continue separating the meat from the entirely flat surface of the scapula on the back side.

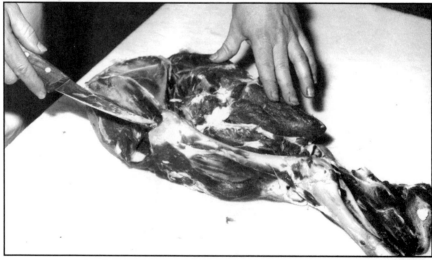

Now turn the shoulder over and separate the remainder of the meat from the wide, flat scapula bone.

The end product is one large, flat slab of shoulder meat with a smaller, almost detached segment constituting the lower leg meat which, again, should be cut free and tossed into the burger bowl.

It is now necessary to set aside this large slab of meat and remove the opposite foreleg and shoulder from the carcass in order to obtain a comparable slab of shoulder meat from that side of the deer.

Now take the two identical slabs of shoulder meat and, insides facing each other, lay one on top of the other. Form them somewhat with your hands to create a nice-looking, football-shaped roast.

Tying the roast is the next step, and a few tricks of the trade will make

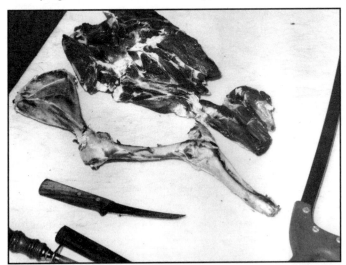

When finished, you should have one large slab of boneless meat. Here, the remaining shoulder bone is shown for an anatomical reference.

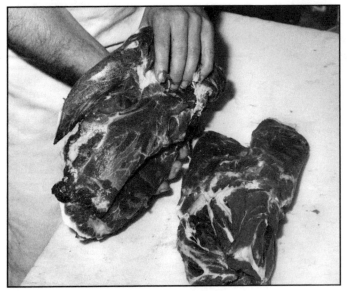

Momentarily set your slab of boned shoulder meat aside, remove the second front leg from the deer carcass, and bone it out in the same manner. This produces two large slabs of shoulder meat that can be placed on top of each other.

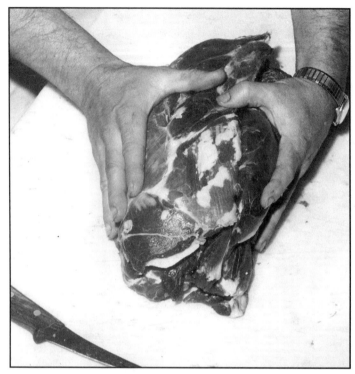

Use your hands to form a single large shoulder roast from the two slabs of boneless meat, then tie the works together with cotton string.

it quite easy. Use cotton string (never nylon) and the so-called surgeon's knot. This is basically a common square knot, but with one exception. Instead of two double-overhand ties, you first make a triple-overhand tie followed by a conventional double-overhand tie. When snugged up against the meat, the triple-overhand will grab it tightly and hold it in place, and won't come loose when you release a bit of tension on the string to make the double-overhand tie to complete the knot.

Another tip is to make your first two string ties at opposite ends of the roast. This will serve to hold the two slabs of shoulder meat firmly together into the shape you've formed; you can then make subsequent string ties moving progressively toward the middle of the roast. Conversely, if you were to instead make the first string tie in the middle of the roast, it would tend to compress the two meat slabs in such a way as to force them out to the opposite sides, which would result in a long, slender, tube-like roast instead of a more desirable thick, plump one.

When all of your string ties are completed (about ten should be sufficient), trim the ends of the roast so it looks neat and toss these end-scraps into the burger pile. Then trim the ends of the string ties to about one-half inch in length.

You now have a professional-looking rolled shoulder roast of venison. If you have a large family (six to eight), this roast can be wrapped for the

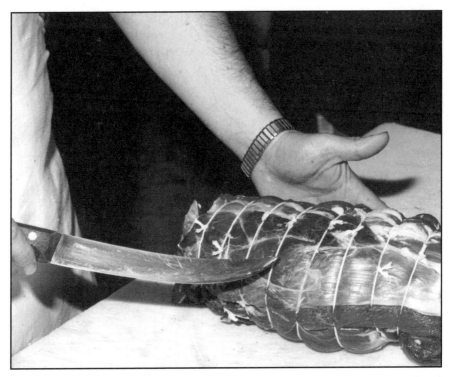

The finished rolled shoulder roast weighs about ten pounds and can easily be reduced to two or three smaller roasts by simply slicing down between the string ties. End pieces and other small "mistakes" can be trimmed away to go into the burger pile.

freezer, as is, in one piece for a future meal. For a smaller family, you can slice it in half right down the middle, between two of the string ties, to give two medium-sized roasts.

Final Words

Never make a very small shoulder roast or try to reduce a large one to a smaller one that would be less than two pounds in weight. This is a common mistake made by hunters when there are only two or three people in the family. The result is a roast that sees the marbling quickly melt and cook away, causing the meat from that point on until it reaches doneness to become dried out and tough. You need a somewhat large or medium-sized roast whose bulk will help the meat retain its internal basting moisture, and therefore tenderness, through the duration of the cooking.

With a small family, this obviously means there may be a good quantity of meat left over when the meal is done. But this does not mean the venison will be wasted, because the remains can be cubed and added to soups and stews. You can also slice it thin and create delicious hot or cold sandwiches.

The last step in butchering the shoulder and leg meat is to go back over the bones with a small knife to remove any additional meat remnants, salvaging these tender tidbits found closest to the bone but missed by your knife, on behalf of the meat grinder.

See how easy it is to become an expert meatcutter? In fact, it's worth mentioning that my friend Charlie Hause, who wielded the knife while I operated the camera, produced the shoulder roast shown here in less time than it took you to read this particular chapter.

10

Butchering the Hind Legs

At the beginning of the previous chapter I mentioned that there is no particular sequence in which butchering various parts of a deer must be undertaken. I then started off describing how to butcher the front legs, and with good reason. Anatomically, they're the easiest, and so this gives the hunter a feel for his work—gets him started—and makes him feel comfortable with the job at hand, all of which reduces his head-scratching time and thus adds to his level of proficiency.

Removing the rear legs from the carcass is slightly more difficult because the haunches are attached to the pelvic girdle by means of a ball and socket. Moreover, the pelvis itself presents many irregularly shaped contours that must be blindly followed with the knife blade to separate muscle from bone.

So I still hold by the statement that you can butcher-out the various deer parts in any sequence you wish. But someone who is a beginner to all of this is well-advised to begin with the easier front legs; once he has several deer-butchering sessions under his belt, he may choose to vary his routine.

In starting work on the back legs, many hunters prefer to use their saw to cut the spine, horizontally, in the region of the small of the back, just before the hams, whereupon both rear legs, still joined by the pelvis, are allowed to fall free. Then they carry the awkward, two-legged hunk to the butcher table and saw down vertically between the two, through the Aitch bone, to separate the legs.

But know in advance you're making far more work for yourself than necessary, because once you have each hind leg on the cutting table, you still have to bone it out and remove the meat from that half-side of the pelvis. Why not simply eliminate the aforementioned effort and, right from the start, cut the leg from its attachment, leaving the pelvis attached to the skeleton.

Start at the root of the tail and begin cutting down through the meat on the left side of the spine to initiate removal of the left leg. Always use just the tip of your boning knife and try to keep the flat blade as close to bone as possible to minimize lost meat; technically, no meat is ever "lost," because when small goofs are committed, as they inevitably are by all of us, the quality of the growing burger pile is enhanced with the tender addition of rump-meat scraps. In any event, you may wish to occasionally use your hands to pull the leg away from the body to somewhat enlarge your work area and better see what you're doing.

As you continue to cut down and around the ham, allow your knife blade to gently travel over the irregular surfaces of the pelvic girdle; when you hit bone, adjust the angle of the blade edge just a bit inward or outward to allow the knife to continue onward through adjacent meat. In time you'll come to the ball and socket assembly, but there is no need to do any bone cutting here. The ball sits loosely in the socket, attached only by a small piece of cartilage. If you slip just the tip of your knife blade down into and between the ball and socket, you can easily cut the cartilage and the leg will begin to fall almost entirely free at this point, requiring just a bit more meat-cutting in the vicinity of the Aitch bone.

Back at the Cutting Table, Again

With the left leg now separated from the carcass and on the work table, once again spend a few minutes getting the meat ready for cutting as you did with each of the front legs. Trim away the large portions of surface tallow, most of which will be high on the leg where it was previously attached to the spinal/pelvic region. Then trim off the thin, protective "rind" or dark-colored casing, which the surface of the venison acquired during aging. After this, go over the entire leg with a damp rag to remove any stray hairs or other debris.

If you wish, you can now use your knife and saw to cut away the lower leg just above the knee. The standard procedure is to first use a knife to cut down through the meat around the diameter of the leg, then use the saw to cut the bone. As with the front legs, the lower sections of the rear legs are laced with sinew and therefore have no use other than feeding your meat grinder.

Cutting the Steaks and Roasts

Now let's get down to the nitty-gritty. The rear leg is composed of three adjoining muscles. Due to their odd shapes the tissue fibers run in somewhat different directions, but there is a thin membrane that covers and unites the three into a whole.

Consequently, there are two ways to butcher the rear leg, depending upon the types of meat cuts you'd like to obtain. You can remove the thin membrane covering the entire haunch and separate the three exposed muscles to produce three roasts (two rump roasts and a sirloin tip roast); or, you

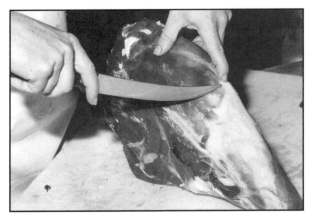

With a back leg separated from the carcass and now on the cutting table, most hunters prefer to first remove the sirloin tip section. After propping the leg up, find the tip of the white knuckle bone as your starting point.

can remove only that part of the membrane covering the sirloin tip in order to remove it (which you can then use as a roast or slice vertically into sirloin tip steaks), but leave the membrane intact on the remaining two muscles and slice them into round steaks.

There is no right or wrong way here, simply a matter of preference as to meat cuts. First remove the sirloin tip by propping up the entire leg on its edge with the lower leg bone facing away from you. You'll easily see the tip of the hard white-knuckle bone and this is your starting point. Cut down through the meat just above the knuckle at a slight angle as shown in the accompanying photo.

After going only a short distance, your knife blade will come to an abrupt halt against the leg bone. Now turn the blade flat and bring the knife cut toward you, keeping the blade continually against the bone until the sirloin tip is cut entirely free.

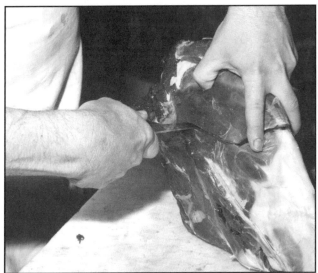

Just forward of the knuckle tip, slice down through the meat until the knife stops against the leg bone. Then turn the blade and, keeping it flat against the leg bone, continue cutting in that direction to remove the entire sirloin tip.

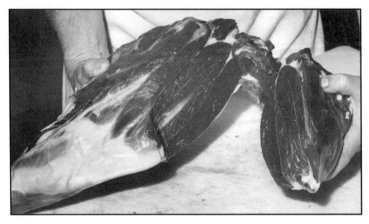

The sirloin tip should come free and entirely intact.

You now have an oblong chunk of solid, boneless meat called the sirloin tip. Easy, huh? You can do either of two things with this football-shaped piece of meat. You can leave it whole, to be cooked as a sirloin tip roast. If this is the case, it's a good idea to tie the roast incrementally along its length, every inch or so, with cotton string as described for roasts from the front shoulder. Since this is very tender meat, it will tend to fall apart during cooking if it's not tied.

You can also vertically slice the meat into about five sirloin tip steaks, each one-inch thick, which are fine for broiling over coals or can be made into Swiss steaks. Since the meat is football shaped, and hence thicker in the middle, you'll end up with steaks of uniform thickness, but those toward either end will be a bit smaller in size than those in the middle. This works out perfectly for dinner guests, who might prefer steaks a bit smaller (or larger) than the others.

Incidentally, the very ends of the sirloin tip have several membrane layers within them, so we usually cut these one-inch pieces free at each end and toss them into the burger pile.

The entire sirloin tip can also be tied with cotton string to produce a three-pound sirloin tip roast. This one has been first layered with bacon to baste the roast as it cooks.

The sirloin tip can now be sliced vertically into about five sirloin tip steaks; the end pieces go into the burger pile.

The next step is the same, regardless of whether you want to use the remainder of the rump for roasts or round steaks. Lay the remaining leg portion with the inside down and the partially exposed leg bone facing you; this is the bone that became exposed when the sirloin tip was removed.

Now remove this entire bone without damaging the meat wrapped around it. Begin by using just the tip of your boning knife to slowly go all the way around its perimeter, gently pulling away the meat as you proceed, and eventually you'll reach the other side. Now make two vertical slices, one to the far left and the other to the far right, to complete the separation of the meat from its attachment at the lower-leg and upper-pelvic regions, and the meat will fall free in one large, boneless slab.

The meat, now without the bone through the middle that previously

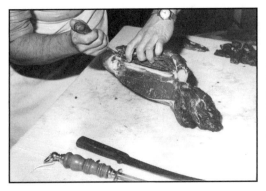

Now go back to the remainder of the hind leg and, using as a guide the exposed bone where the sirloin tip was removed, entirely encircle the bone with your knife to remove the remainder of the rump meat intact.

held everything together, can now be returned to its former shape by molding it with your hands so it looks almost exactly at it did a minute ago. Here is where working with very cold meat pays off in easy handling, compared to meat that is warm, floppy, and difficult to control.

What to do with this large chunk of rump meat? Very popular with many hunters is to simply use a long-bladed butcher knife to slice it vertically into about five one-inch-thick round steaks.

Another way of producing these round steaks is by merely skipping the boning-out procedure just described and, instead, slicing the steaks with the butcher knife down through the meat until the bone is reached, and then cutting the bone with a saw. In this manner, you'll create round steaks that will be the same size and shape, and each will have a disk-like piece of round

The entire slab of rump meat, with the bone removed, can be molded by hand back into its former shape, then sliced vertically to produce about six round steaks. Instead of boning out the meat, some hunters prefer to use a meat saw; the same size round steaks are produced but with a small, round bone in the middle of each.

leg bone in the center. As mentioned previously, I prefer boneless cuts of venison, but the choice is yours.

If you'd like roasts instead of round steaks, that is also a splendid decision because, coming from the rump, they'll be as tender as any cut the deer has to offer. Rolled rump roasts are produced in the same way as rolled shoulder roasts.

Use your hands to shape and form the meat back together so it looks the same as before the leg bone was removed. Now use cotton string to tie the roast in ten or twelve places, beginning at opposite ends and working gradually toward the middle. Once it's secured with string, you can leave the roast whole for a sumptuous repast that will serve eight, or you can slice it in half to produce two meals that each serve four.

Despite his most valiant efforts, any hunter is likely to end up with numerous, smallish chunks of rump meat. The excuse I use is that my knife blade sometimes has a mind of its own. These pieces of meat will predictably be so irregularly shaped and of varied sizes that one will be tempted to reserve them for the meat grinder. That's fine, because it will result in the most delicious burger and sausage imaginable.

On the other hand, keep in mind that burger and sausage are traditionally made from cuts of tougher meat that must be chopped by a grinder's blades, but what you now have is an accumulation of very tender rump meat. Our choice is to wrap and freeze these miscellaneous pieces in one-pound packages. Later, when defrosted, they can be further reduced to one-inch chunks or half-inch thick strips that can be used in stroganoff, stir-fry, and similar recipes that call for tender meat.

The last step is to go over the rear leg bone one more time and clean it thoroughly of the smallest scraps of remaining meat for the burger pile.

Now it's time to move on to the other rear leg and, since you've gained a good deal of practice, the work should go quickly. You can butcher it exactly the same way if you like, or you may decide to do it just a little differently to add variety to your future meals. For example, if you left the sirloin tip intact as a roast, you may wish to use the other one, sliced vertically, for sir-

If you goof and some of the round steaks are not of uniform thickness, a bit of quick work with a meat mallet solves everything.

loin tip steaks. Similarly, if you previously sliced the rump meat into round steaks, you may wish to use the rump meat of the right leg for rolled rump roasts. To each his own pleasure!

Larding and Barding

Before proceeding to other butchering procedures, let's take a few moments to discuss two techniques for tenderizing venison that you may wish to incorporate into meatcutting operations dealing with either the front shoulder roasts or the rump roasts produced from the rear legs.

In earlier chapters we discussed being a selective hunter and what to look for in body conformation that signals tender venison. Sometimes, however, after his deer is down, the hunter may have reason to suspect that the venison is not likely to be as tender as he'd hoped for. This may tempt him to shove the entire deer through the tiny spout of his meat grinder—but wait!

There are two after-the-fact techniques, known as larding and barding, that can be instituted during the butchering of the front and rear legs, that will transform even a grizzled old buck's venison into such tender fare you'll feel compelled to bow your head in reverence as you dine. To understand the benefits of these two techniques, let's once again briefly visit a comparison between domestic livestock and wild game.

Beef steers, for example, spend lives of leisure lazing around pastures and

In finishing the butchering of a rear leg, there will be several large chunks of rump meat left over. The largest can be assembled into rolled rump roasts and tied with cotton string. The smallest are prime rump meat. We don't use them for burger, but cut them into chunks for later use in stews, stir fries, and meat casseroles.

feedlots awaiting their destiny and seldom utilizing their muscles to the fullest extent of their physical capability. And, all the while, they dine complacently upon assorted high-fat and high-carbohydrate foods, which in turn make them quite fatty in their musculature. Additionally, about a month before they are to be slaughtered, they are subjected to a "finishing" process in which they are force-fed milk, and grain such as corn, to even further increase the fat content of their musculature.

The result of this modern animal husbandry is that domestic livestock meat contains a very high level of marbling throughout its flesh. This marbling fat is found in striations between and through the tissue fibers of the meat, and during cooking it melts and subsequently helps to break down (and greatly tenderize) the tissue's cellular structure.

Exactly the opposite sequence of events occurs during the lives of deer. Although they may occasionally lunch at some farmer's cornfield, a majority of the year sees deer dining upon whatever native foods they can find, and often they do not find all that much, particularly during winter. Further, deer spend much of their time on the run, and this continual exercise, as with a human athlete, hardens them off in the building of tough musculature. You just don't see fat, flabby deer and, of course, they do not undergo a finishing process prior to opening day; indeed, when they are taken by hunters they may be in a state of stress and lactic acid build-up.

Consequently, unlike domestic livestock, venison does not possess a high level of marbling. Instead, it is a dry, very lean meat with very little in the way of tissue fat to internally lubricate the meat as it cooks.

There are several ways to remedy this state of affairs. First, as emphasized previously, trim away as much tallow fat as time and convenience allow, but leave whatever marbling fat you find woven between the muscle and tissue fibers. It is easily identified because unlike tallow fat, which is formed in thick layers on the outside surfaces of the meat, marbling appears as long, thin streaks and flecks within the interior of the meat. Second, consider barding the meat. This involves adding fat to the venison.

One method, when you have a large slab of shoulder or rump meat you are preparing to assemble into a roast, is to first lay several slices of bacon in the folds of the meat before forming it into a roast with your hands and tying it with cotton string. This will do a good job of tenderizing the meat, and will also impart a very subtle, yet pleasing, bacon flavor. Instead of using bacon, you can also use thinly cut strips of beef suet or salt pork, each of which will impart their own flavors as well.

Another barding method is to drape the exterior of the roast with bacon strips just before tying it securely with string. As the roast cooks, the bacon will slowly melt and drip-baste the venison.

There are two slight disadvantages to barding, one of which is that the

When rolled roasts are created from either the front or rear legs, and they're from a deer you suspect may not be so tender, use the technique called barding, in which bacon or salt pork is layered between the folds of meat before it is tied. It will melt during cooking and lubricate the meat to tenderness.

hunter does not obtain a pure, unadulterated venison flavor but one of venison slightly accentuated with beef or pork characteristics.

The other drawback is that any kind of beef or pork fat does not keep very long in your freezer, which means that venison roasts that have exterior bacon drapes or interior insertions of bacon, beef suet, or salt pork must be used within several months.

If you desire to conserve your cache of deer meat and make it last as long as possible, you won't want to use barding as a meat-tenderizing technique. So go ahead and produced your rolled, tied roasts as described earlier, and place them in the freezer where they'll remain in good condition for up to two years (believe it or not) if you follow the steps described in the chapter devoted to freezing venison.

Then, each time you remove a roast from the freezer, and just before cooking, use another technique called larding, which accomplishes the very same tenderizing as barding but without the drawback of limited storage time in the freezer. Larding means injecting fat and similar lubricants into the meat by means of an inexpensive larding needle.

As before, you can use bacon, suet, or salt pork, which will impart subtle flavors of their own, but first rendering them down; that is, very slowly cooking them in a pan to reduce them to liquid fat. If you'd prefer to retain the exclusive flavor of the venison, with nothing to detract from it, use a relatively tasteless larding fluid such as melted butter, cooking oil, or a combination of the two mixed together.

A larding needle looks somewhat like a siphon, in that a rubber squeeze bulb is fitted to one end of a stainless-steel tube, with a long, hollow needle at the other. Simply squeeze the bulb to expel its air, insert the needle into the larding liquid, release the pressure on the bulb, and it will suck in as much larding fluid as the bulb will hold. Then insert the needle in random locations

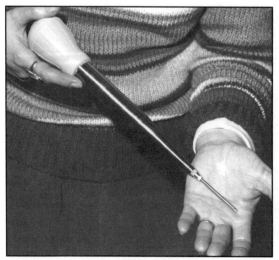

in the meat, briefly squeeze the bulb, and the larding fluid will saturate the inside of the roast.

If you're in camp or some other location, and a larding needle is not available, use a long, narrow knife blade to pierce numerous holes into the roast and then use the tip of the blade to insert slivers of bacon or salt pork.

Another technique for tenderizing roasts from the front and rear legs is larding, using a larding needle. The utensil is filled with melted butter, bacon fat, or cooking oil and injected into the roast in random locations.

11

Butchering Loins and Ribs

You can refer to them as loins, tenderloins, steaks, backstraps, or other common names, but by any description they are the tenderest cuts of venison a deer possesses. They are located along both sides of the backbone. If they're on the underneath sides of the spine within the chest cavity, they're most correctly, in the case of deer, referred to as tenderloins; their counterparts on a beef steer are called filet mignons.

If they're located on the top, exterior sides of the spine, just beneath the hide, they're most correctly, in the case of deer referred to as backstraps; their counterparts on a beef steer are simply referred to as different types of steaks such as porterhouse steaks, which have the filet mignon present, or T-bone steaks, in which the filet mignon has been cut away.

There are several ways to remove these delectable cuts of venison, depending upon whether you like pure, boneless steak meat or whether you prefer bone-in steaks.

If you'll recall, in an earlier chapter I suggested the tenderloins be removed, and how to do it, shortly after the field-dressed animal arrives at camp or home. The tenderloins are so tender that they require no aging whatever; and besides, they are relatively small in size, and after even a brief exposure to air they quickly develop a hard, glazed surface that must be trimmed away, at the sacrifice of a good deal of prime meat.

The backstraps, on the exterior of

When a hunter takes a beautiful buck like this, he's first captivated by the antlers. Then his attention turns to the deer's most tender cut, the backstrap steaks. (photo by Northern Wildlife Ventures)

The backstraps lie on either side of the spine and are easily filleted right out of their triangular-shaped pockets. This hunter is working on the tenderloin steaks, also found along both sides of the spine but inside the chest cavity.

the skeletal system, lie adjacent to the backbone, running from just behind the front shoulder back to where the front of the rear legs begin. They're situated in a type of triangular-shaped pocket created by the offset vertebrae of the backbone.

Removing the backstraps intact, in long strips, is accomplished by using a fillet knife or boning knife with a flexible tip that will easily bend to conform to the curvature of the bones. Insert the tip of your blade just behind the front shoulder and, with the blade flat against the backbone, carefully guide it all the way along the length of the spine to just above the pelvic girdle where you made your first incision in the removal of the back leg on that side. It will feel at times as if the blade is traveling over a rippled surface (these are the vertebrae), so proceed slowly and work the blade slightly in and out as you go along in order to retain as much meat as possible.

Now, back at that point where you began the shoulder cut, make another

Each backstrap weighs about eight pounds; it is pure, boneless meat that is easily and quickly butchered.

cut, this time perpendicular, about four inches in length. Then it is quite simple to cut and lift, cut and lift, gently filleting the backstrap right out of its spinal pocket until its entire length is removed. Then do exactly the same on the opposite side of the spinal column to remove its strip of backstrap meat.

At the butchering table you'll notice a thin, silvery-colored membrane-like sheath covering the exterior of the backstrap. You can trim this away with your knife, if you wish, by starting at one end and alternately lifting the membrane while running the flat of the blade between it and the meat. However, this operation is merely for the sake of appearance; it is not necessary because the membrane, also called silverskin, will cook out as very tender.

Next, you'll want to slice the lengthy backstrap horizontally into numerous steaks. On a very large deer, which in turn will have large backstraps, you can simply begin slicing the steaks any thickness you prefer (I recommend from one to two inches thick).

Most hunters prefer to slice their backstraps into one-inch-thick steaks. If desired, however, you can butterfly them as shown to produce larger portions.

However, when a deer is only average size, this technique results in the sliced steaks being rather small, and so I use the butterfly method of cutting them. In this procedure, you begin slicing a steak of the desired thickness but do not cut all the way down through the meat. Now, make a second cut another inch or so away, and this time do slice all the way through. What you'll have, then, is a pair of steaks side by side, connected to each other by a type of hinge that, when the steaks are opened and laid out flat, produces a steak double the usual size.

As you approach either end of the long backstrap it will become progressively smaller in size, so begin making your cuts just a bit thicker. Then use a wooden mallet to gently pound them out flat. This will spread out their surface areas somewhat, so that all the steaks from the backstrap are of uniform size, rather than some small and some large.

You can also leave the eight-inch-long end cuts intact and freeze them whole. We like to place these on a grill and slice them very thin at the table, as in chateaubriand, or to make steak sandwiches.

The other meatcutting method for the backstraps, which produces bone-in steaks (some hunters call them chops), requires considerably more work, but the procedure is easily described.

A third option is to cut the entire backstrap into only four lengthy sections of about two pounds a piece, to be grilled whole or baked.

Begin by sawing the deer lengthwise into two halves, down the centerline of the backbone. This is done before butchering-out the hind legs, as the two rear legs left intact can allow the carcass to remain hanging from the gambrel; once the deer is in halves, each hind leg can then be removed and dealt with as described in the previous chapter, leaving the remainder of the backbone halves and their attached backstraps. Next, each side is simply laid upon the cutting table and steaks are vertically sawed to whatever thickness you prefer. Then the rib ends, which contain very little meat, are removed.

If you harbor doubts as to which method you might like best, here's a good suggestion: try both. Halve the deer down the centerline and saw steaks bone-in, and then on the opposite side of the backbone fillet-out the boneless backstrap intact.

As mentioned in a previous chapter, the tenderloins found against either side of the backbone but inside the chest cavity are generally left in whole condition when removed, to be cooked intact in a variety of ways, such as grilling.

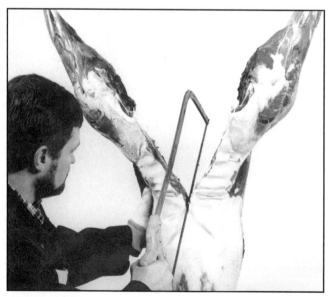

Instead of boneless backstrap steaks, some hunters prefer bone-in steaks, commonly called chops. After the front legs are removed, saw the carcass in half lengthwise down through the middle of the spine. After the rear legs are cut free, the so-called saddle is then sawed horizontally into steaks.

Final Meatcutting Tasks

All that should now remain on your deer carcass is the neck meat, ribs, and brisket meat. The neck meat has many uses. Remove it from the carcass by boning it out. The easiest method is to begin at the back of the neck with a horizontal cut just below the ears, and another one just above the shoulder. Then make a lengthwise cut down the centerline on one side of the neckbone or the other. Make it a deep cut as this will produce a large flap of neck meat and simultaneously expose the neck bone, allowing you to easily continue working around its perimeter.

With the slab of neck meat on your cutting table, remove as much surface tallow as possible, but retain the more deeply imbedded marbling fat. This large slab of meat can now be rolled into a large roast and tied with string, then halved or even cut into thirds for very slow cooking over low heat (as in a crockpot) for six or eight hours. Or, you can cube the neck meat for use in stews. Or, you can reserve the entire quantity of neck meat for burger and sausage.

Only the forward two-thirds of the rib-plate, closest to the neck and measuring about a foot long and half again as wide, is worth cutting out and saving; farther back, there's so little meat on the bones it's hardly worth working for.

Many hunters don't care for venison ribs, saying the meat contains so much tallow that it's like chewing a mouthful of paste. The trick to eliminating this problem is to pre-cook the ribs. That is, place them on a slotted broiler pan and slip them under the broiler at just a medium-heat setting for about forty-five minutes. This will cause the tallow to melt and drain away into the bottom of the broiler-pan assembly. From that point on, you can proceed with any rib recipe you like, such as basting them with barbecue sauce on a charcoal grill, slow-cooking them in a crockpot, or slow-cooking them in a baking pan in the oven . . . all with tender, delectable results.

Other hunters take still another approach to using their ribs. Using a knife, they cut the rib meat free from between the bones comprising the rib cage and add it to their accumulated pile of burger and sausage trimmings but slightly reducing the quantity of beef fat or pork those recipes call for, as described in the next two chapters.

The meat on the brisket has many uses, such as going into burger or sausage; when removing it in a slab with the flat of your knife against the lower-front chest region, be sure to trim away as much surface tallow and cod fat as possible.

As with the neck meat, that of the brisket meat is especially well-suited to being cut into inch-thick chunks and used as the main ingredient in stews. Both the neck and brisket meat are flavorful but also quite tough, which is actually to their advantage. You want stew meat to hold together well during long hours of slow simmering but eventually become tender. Brisket and neck meat do this very well. Conversely, trying to make stew from already tender cuts of venison such as rump meat is often futile. By the time it has slowly cooked for several hours over low heat, the meat no longer is firm and something you can sink your teeth into, but mushy and fallen apart.

About this time, all that should remain of your deer carcass is a skeleton that has been picked clean, without even an ounce remaining that isn't at least suitable for burger and sausage.

Undoubtedly, however, as you've been carrying out your butchering you'll have accumulated a hefty quantity of skin remnants, junk meats, and other trimmings that are too fatty or too sinewy to be used for human consumption. Instead of throwing them away, they make splendid dog food.

In fact, whenever we first begin butchering a deer we always place a five-gallon pot on the stove, half filled with water and turned on low heat. We toss any undesirable meat scraps into the pot as we go along. This "stew" slowly simmers for many hours, to the point that even the gristle becomes tender.

We usually end up with as much as forty pounds of nutritious, high-protein food our dogs absolutely love. After the food has cooked, allow it to cool, then ladle it into half-quart plastic containers (the type in which cottage cheese is sold). Every few days, defrost one container, heat it up a bit, and then mix it with your dog's usual dry kibbles. He'll attack the meal as if there's no tomorrow, especially if it's bitter cold outside.

Not only do you save a lot of money making this dog food, but you gain the satisfaction of knowing you utilized the entire deer, throwing away nothing but bones.

12

How to Grind Burger

A t one time, long ago, I looked down my nose at those hunters who transformed their entire deer into burger and sausage. I thought they were ignorant clods who never took the time to learn the proper way to butcher their deer into steaks and roasts. It seemed they preferred to take the easy way out by simply whacking off the carcass meat in chunks and shreds, not caring how pitiful it appeared because it soon would all be turned into ground meat anyway.

Then I met Harvey Wilks, a Cleveland deer hunter who changed my opinion. Wilks has sometimes been known to filch a single backstrap from his deer and place the whole thing on a charcoal grill for a family cookout, but generally the entire animal goes through his grinder.

"A number of years ago we started paying closer attention to our health, and in our diets we became concerned about all the chemicals, additives, preservatives, and artificial coloring agents being added to foods," Wilks explained. "There were so many of these, especially on the labels of sausage packages, we wondered where they found the room to put the meat! So I started making venison burger and sausage. We found them even more delicious than their store-bought counterparts and, just as important, we knew exactly which ingredients went in, and which did not."

As to the decision to use the whole deer in this manner, Wilks describes his philosophy this way:

"There are various grades of quality in burger and sausage. And so, naturally, that which includes all the hams and loin-cuts is going to be far superior to that which is made only from the neck, lower legs, and other lesser body parts."

Like most families, Harvey Wilks and his wife and kids consume quite a lot of ground meat during the year, which further justifies his personal decisions as to how a deer is to be processed.

"In addition to burger for sandwiches, we frequently have meatloaf and meatballs, and the rest of the burger is incorporated into chili or sauces to go along with spaghetti, lasagna, marzetti, and various types of casseroles."

In the sausage department, Wilks begins by making bulk sausage to be used for sandwiches, breakfast patties, pizza toppings, and casseroles. But he doesn't stop there. Next, he makes link sausages such as kielbasa, Polish sausage, summer sausage, and sometimes even salami, bologna, and pepperoni. No wonder he needs to use the whole deer!

What, then, is a hunter to do if he wants to follow Harvey Wilks' lead? How can one possibly stash in his freezer a year's worth of good eating in the form of steaks, roasts, and stew meat plus burger and several varieties of sausage to meet a family's needs during the year?

Well, you can't. And that alone is a good enough reason to hunt often enough to take more than one deer per year, and to also get other family members interested in hunting.

Meat-Grinding Equipment for You

Meat grinders are available these days in a wide variety of brand names, sizes, prices, and quality. The least expensive and, ironically enough, one of the most durable, is a cast-iron hand-crank model that's available in any houseware department.

By means of a thumb-screw, you clamp it onto the edge of a table or work counter. Meat trimmings are then fed into the top mouth of the

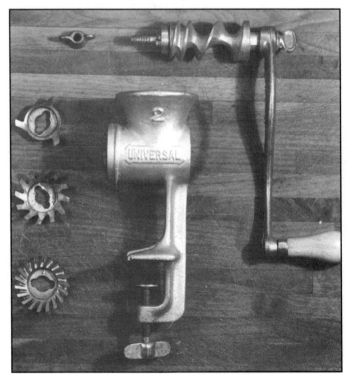

A hand-crank grinder clamps onto the edge of a table and is durable enough for a lifetime of use. Interchangeable blades allow for coarse, medium, or fine grinds.

grinder and the handle turned. The front of the grinder has a removable faceplate, underneath which can be installed interchangeable disks with holes of various sizes. There also is a three- or four-bladed cutting knife. This arrangement allows a hunter to coarse-grind the meat first, then feed it through the grinder a second or even third time to produce burger or bulk sausage of various textures. To make link sausage, as I'll detail in the next chapter, a long spout is attached to the front of the grinder and the meat force-fed into casings. The main drawback to a hand-crank grinder is that it can take an inordinate length of time and muscle power to process many pounds of venison.

The next category of meat grinders includes intermediate-sized electric models produced by the major appliance makers. I have both good words and bad words about them. Their prices range from about $125 to $250, and they operate under the same basic principles as the hand-crank models with the exception that a 110-volt motor does the work instead of you and in far less time. For hunters who like to savor steaks and roasts from their deer and therefore plan to make only modest quantities of burger and sausage (less than twenty-five pounds per year), these grinders are worthwhile investments. Realize, however, these grinders are not intended for, or built to withstand, heavy-duty use. They are countertop kitchen appliances with the homemaker in mind who might occasionally find need to grind small quantities of meat. If you try to cram an entire deer through one of these machines, it will moan and groan, and then it will shudder and squeal and shut down. I was once given one of these grinders as a gift, and over a time span of only two months it succeeded in chewing up only about seventy-five pounds of meat before finally self-destructing. Considering the price of the grinder, we dined on very expensive burger that year.

Then, there are still larger table-model electric grinders made by those companies that manufacture commercial grade equipment. Instead of being rated by voltage, their electric motors are stated in horsepower ratings. Their prices range from $400 to $900 and the most popular motor sizes are one-third, one-half, and three-quarter horsepower.

I can't praise these heavy-duty, table-model grinders enough. They're ruggedly built because they are intended for use by farmers who annually slaughter a couple of beef steers and hogs for their family's use, as well as for restaurants, small grocery stores, and delis, so you know they will serve admirably in the processing of as many deer per year as you may harvest. To give an idea as to how efficient these grinders are, those with one-half-horsepower motors will process an average of three pounds of meat per minute. And they will continue working hour after hour, without showing any signs of fatigue.

To be sure, it's unreasonable to expect some hunters to cough-up $500 or more for a meat grinder when they didn't even pay that much for their firearm. But consider this: such a grinder will easily last the rest of your life. No kidding. These grinders are designed to work hard for twenty-five years with little or no maintenance; at that time, after paying a modest amount for an overhaul, you can expect still another twenty-five years of service. They simply live on and on. Moreover, the machines are a real pleasure to use, not only in the processing of venison but many other types of food preparation as well. In this light, their per-year-use-cost is quite low.

Hunters who normally take more than one deer per year often invest in an electric, tabletop grinder that will process three pounds of meat per minute.

However, don't expect to find these quality grinders sitting on the shelves with the El Cheapo models in a local department store. You usually have to go to a restaurant supply company. There's at least one in every major city; check the phone book's Yellow Pages. Also check a newspaper's classified ads because restaurants, delis, and mom & pop grocery stores periodically sell their equipment; it's undoubtedly still in excellent condition, but if mom and pop's business is booming, they may need to upgrade to a larger model with greater grinding capacity.

The only regular service a meat grinder requires—whether it is a hand-crank or electric model—is cleaning. After each use, disassemble the grinder's hopper, feed screw, and cutting blade and wash them in hot soapy water. Of course, never submerge an electric grinder's motor in water; just wipe down the outside of the housing with a damp cloth.

Before putting the grinder away, ensure that the metal meatcutting parts do not rust by giving them a light coat of vegetable cooking oil. In the event that you retrieve your grinder from its storage place after several months of nonuse and discover light scale rust on the inner surfaces of many parts, the standard procedure for cleaning the parts before use is to run a handful or two of saltine crackers through the grinder. The abrasive nature of the salt, and the absorptive nature of the crackers, will restore the grinder's bare metal surfaces to a bright shine in a minute or so.

Let's Grind

Producing your own burger is enjoyable, easy work, and anyone can do a professional job on the very first attempt.

Before actually grinding the venison, it's necessary to acquire a quantity of beef suet or beef fat. How much you need depends upon how much burger you plan to make. The recommended ratio is three parts venison to one part suet or fat.

With deer hunting seasons now lasting several months in most states, and hunters commonly taking two

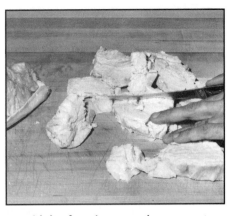

As with beef, venison must have some type of fat added to moisturize the ground meat and make it tender. Beef fat or beef suet is recommended. Begin by cutting it into chunks that will fit into the feeder mouth of your grinder.

or more deer per year, there often is a run on suet and fat during the season. Because of this, consider how much burger you'd like to make during the season, and then place a pre-season order with the meat department of your local grocery store. If the whole deer were to be used for burger, you'd need about twenty-five pounds of fat or suet; with that in mind, you should be able to estimate proportionately smaller amounts.

Beef suet is comparable to the tallow found on deer and consists of the thick, hard, white, lardy fat found in layers around the kidneys, down both sides of the back, and across the rump. It costs so little—usually less than twenty-five cents per pound—that if you're a regular customer, your butcher may give the stuff to you for free.

Beef fat, on the other hand, lies closer to the carcass meat, beneath the suet, and therefore is not quite so thick and lardy; it's the excess fat butchers remove during their final trimming around steaks and other loin cuts. If there is any cost at all for beef-fat trimmings, the price will be about the same as suet.

Since beef fat is more tender and flakier than suet, it makes better burger, in my opinion, although the actual difference may be more imagined than real. So try to get beef fat trimmings, but if you can't, suet will be fine.

Prior to beginning your meat grinding, you'll want to make sure your venison is very cold so that the blade in your grinder can cut the meat crisply and cleanly. If the meat is at room temperature, it will have a tendency to mush. I usually take care of major butchering operations one day, then allow my accumulated meat scraps to sit overnight in a covered bowl in my refrigerator and commence grinding the following day. However, if you want to process the entire deer in one day, spread your intended burger meat out on trays or cookie sheets and place them in your freezer for fifteen minutes or until they are thoroughly chilled.

Meanwhile, as your burger meat is chilling, begin cutting up your suet or beef fat into thumb-sized chunks. These will go through the grinder much faster and easier than big globs of the lardy suet, which in time will only serve to clog the grinder. If the feed screw and other parts do become clogged with a thick, pasty layer that is beginning to retard the operation of the machine (this is more common with hand-crank rather than electric models), simply remove those parts and, using tongs, hold them briefly under a stream of very hot tap water; all the fat residue will dissolve and wash away almost instantly, whereupon you can quickly reassemble the parts and pick up where you left off.

The suet, or beef fat, after passing through the coarse grinding plate, will come out of the grinder's exit flange looking somewhat like "crumbles," for want of a better term. Just accumulate them in a large tray or bowl.

Next, run your suet or beef fat through your grinder's coarse plate, then set the fat bits aside.

Now feed your chilled venison through the same coarse plate, remembering again to feed small golfball-sized pieces through the grinder rather than huge chunks.

Although some hunters use a baby scale to obtain the desired three-to-one ratio of venison to suet with unerring accuracy, the truth of the matter is that this is nothing more than needless busywork. Being precisely accurate isn't imperative. Since venison and suet have about the same weight-to-volume density, it's easy to make a visual estimate of three parts venison to one part suet or beef fat and come so close to the desired proportions that you'll never notice the difference between one batch and another.

After the suet and venison have each been ground separately through your coarse grinding plate, the next step is to spread the venison out on a large flat work surface. On top of it, sprinkle your beef fat or suet "crumbles."

Now run your accumulated venison scraps and trimmings through the grinder's coarse plate.

Then thoroughly knead the two together with your hands until they are well mixed.

This accomplished, remove the coarse grinding plate and insert the medium grinding plate and run your burger through the mill again. It will probably now be of exactly the appearance and consistency you like, appearing almost identical to store-bought burger. But if desired, the mixture can be run through the grinder a third time to produce a still-finer texture.

On a large, flat work surface such as a chopping block table, use your hands to mix together the ground fat and venison.

Now run your burger mixture through your grinder again, this time through the medium grinding plate.

The finished burger is lean and delicious and can be used in any way that you might use beef hamburger.

Any burger you desire to use will stay in good condition in your refrigerator for three days. The remainder should be wrapped for the freezer.

Call it deerburger, buckburger, hamburger, or whatever you like, but it can be used in exactly the same way as you'd use conventional store-bought burger. Nevertheless, toward the end of the book I've included some long-time favorite recipes of my own and friends.

13

How to Grind Bulk Sausage and Make Links

aking sausage has always held a mystical attraction reminiscent of bygone days, closely guarded family secrets, and
a padlock on the smokehouse door. But we're going to
dispel with that mystery and show you how simple the
procedure really is.

You've already made burger and have seen how quickly and easily it can
be done. Making sausage is essentially the same, with two minor exceptions.
In addition to grinding together a mixture of venison and beef fat, you add
a third ingredient . . . lean pork. I prefer buying inexpensive pork butt or pork
shoulder that later, at home, is trimmed of most of its rind or fat. Then,
between the first and second grinding operations, you sprinkle the meat with
seasonings. I told you it was easy!

Needed Equipment

The meat grinder you previously used for making burger is likewise perfect
for making sausage in bulk form. However, if you'd like to also make link
sausage or ring sausage, you'll need an accessory attachment . . . a casing
stuffer. This is nothing more than an inexpensive plastic spout that fits on the
front of your grinder. If one of these gizmos wasn't included with your
grinder when you bought it, check the owner's manual and undoubtedly you
can order one. If not, go to a restaurant supply company and obtain a universal casing link stuffer that fits most brands of meat grinders; it should cost
less than five dollars.

Bulk Sausage

The meat-blending ratio for all venison sausage is three-to-one-to-one.
In other words, to obtain five pounds of sausage you'd mix together three

The same equipment used for grinding burger, either electric or hand-operated, can be adapted to making bulk venison sausage. If you also want to make sausage links, all you need is an accessory stuffing spout that fits onto the front of the machine.

Feed each of the three meats through the coarse plate of your grinder, then knead the three meats together with your hands and grind a second time through the medium plate.

pounds of venison, one pound of beef fat, and one pound of pork.

Begin by grinding each of the meats separately. As with burger, the meat should be quite cold, and small chunks will go through the cutting blade much faster than large globs.

After running each of the three meats through the grinder's coarse plate, thoroughly knead them together with your hands and then run the mixture through the grinder a second time, now using the medium grinding plate.

You now have basic bulk sausage. But wait! Now we have to season the meat, so spread the sausage over a large work area such as a chopping-block table or countertop.

The characteristic flavors of different types of sausage are obtained by blending various seasonings, spices, and aromatic seeds. You can custom blend your own ingredients by consulting any of the endless number of books devoted exclusively to making sausage. But I recommend you first try a commercially prepared sausage-seasoning mix. These come in paper envelopes and are available in most grocery stores and meat markets; most are put up in four-ounce and eight-ounce

Use a prepared seasoning mix the first time you make sausage. Grocery stores have many variations from which to choose.

quantities, which are sufficient for producing twelve pounds or twenty-five pounds of sausage, respectively.

These sausage seasonings vary enormously in their component ingredients. Even the same company may have numerous, slight variations that they distribute to stores in different ethnic neighborhoods. For example, in a predominantly Italian community, the sausage-seasoning packets, no matter what type of sausage is to be made, are sure to have fennel spice and garlic as two main ingredients (among many others). In Scandinavian regions, you'll find fennel and sage. And in Spanish, Mexican American, and Hispanic regions you'll find red cayenne pepper, sage, and cumin. There is not a Hungarian or Slovakian sausage recipe that does not possess paprika, and popular German sausages typically have heavy dosages of black pepper, allspice, cloves, and nutmeg. In each case, uniquely different flavors are achieved and over several centuries have served as tasty hallmarks distinguishing different nationalities. Still other seasonings commonly found in sausage include salt, white pepper, sugar, dry mustard, thyme, rosemary, marjoram, bay leaves, ginger, and mace.

So my advice is to peruse the selection available in various stores and buy just a few prepared seasoning mixes at first, making only small quantities of sausage using each. Then decide which particular ones you and your family like and which you don't care for. This is really the only logical way to

Many hunters like to make venison sausage in a variety of forms and with many different ethnic seasonings.

season sausage, because we all come from different backgrounds and have taste preferences.

Going back to your work surface covered with sausage mix and your packet of prepared seasoning in hand, here's one word of caution. Don't simply dump the seasoning onto the sausage mix. Scrounge around your cupboard for a seldom-used saltshaker and fill it with the seasoning mix; or take a small glass jar and punch

holes in the lid. Then sprinkle the seasoning over the sausage to ensure an even distribution rather than spotty places of under or over saturation. With the seasoning applied, in accordance with the prescribed quantity on the packet's instruction label, now knead the meat thoroughly with your hands.

At this point, many people like to place their sausage mix in a large, covered bowl in the refrigerator overnight, believing this grace period allows the spices and herbs to completely meld with each other and permeate the meat before it is pushed through the grinder a final time. I've

To uniformly season the sausage, spread the mix out onto a large work surface and then use an old salt shaker to evenly sprinkle on the seasoning. Briefly knead the sausage mix through the medium plate and refrigerate overnight before cooking or freezing.

tried both ways, letting the sausage age overnight, or immediately going onto the next step, and honestly can't tell the difference in the final product.

In either case, the last step is to run the sausage mixture through the medium-coarse plate of your grinder a final time, and then to wrap and label individual packages of your bulk sausage for the freezer.

Stuffing Sausage Links and Rings

As good as it is, many hunters, after they've produced bulk sausage, like to practice the more refined art of stuffing it into casings.

You can obtain either synthetic or natural casings, depending upon your preferences. Synthetic casings have an indefinite storage life, they cook out quite tender, and they look quite pleasing, just as if you had a custom butcher make your sausages. The drawback is that they're quite expensive and may be difficult to find.

Natural casings don't cook out nearly so tender and yield a definite skin-like covering on the sausages. They also are limited in their storage life, and the final appearance of your sausages will often take on a distinct "down on the farm" look. Yet natural casings are readily available and inexpensive.

Natural casings, of course, are the intestines of sheep, hogs, or beef steers.

In a packinghouse they are removed from the animal, turned inside-out, thoroughly cleaned and sanitized, and then packed in either coarse dry salt or a brine solution.

The smallest casings come from sheep and are primarily used in the making of breakfast sausages, wieners, and pepperoni; these are the most tender casings you can buy. Slightly larger in size, and the most commonly used, are hog casings, which typically are stuffed as polish sausage, kielbasa, and the like. The looped sections of beef steer intestines are the largest casings and they are used in making ring bologna and salami. The middle sections of beef steer intestines—called "straights"—are used in making summer sausage. Since beef steer intestines are quite tough, they are later almost always peeled away and not eaten.

I'll describe here the use of hog casings, simply because that's what a majority of deer-hunting sausage makers seem to prefer. The techniques that apply to the use of sheep and beef casings, either natural or synthetic, are the same; only their sizes differ, and therefore the sizes of the stuffing spouts required of them.

Casings can be purchased through most large chain-grocery stores and meat markets, or they can order them for you. One pound of hog casings is sufficient to stuff one hundred pounds of venison sausage. Now here's the glitch. In most cases you'll require only four or six ounces of casings but most suppliers don't want to deal with such small quantities and generally put them up in two-pound packages; that's enough to turn three entire deer into sausage! The solution is twofold. You can store leftover casings in your refrigerator for a year if they remain in their salt or brine packing, or if you don't want to hold them over until next year you can share them with deer-hunting partners who want to make their own sausage.

When preparing to make sausage links or rings, don't try to handle long lengths of the casings at one time. Use scissors to snip off several sections at a time, each about four feet long.

Before using the casings, you have to first rinse them with running water

Sausage casings, available at the meat sections of grocery stores, come bulk-packed in a brine preservative.

Before using casings to make link sausage, flush out their insides with water to remove all traces of their salt preservatives.

to remove all traces of their salt preservative. Pay particular attention to flushing out the insides of the casings by simply taking one end and slipping it over the mouth of your sink faucet. Be careful! At first the casings are slippery, and if you drop one it will slide right down the drain; to prevent this from happening, lay a terrycloth towel in the bottom of the sink.

After washing the casings, allow them to soak in a bowl of lukewarm water for about twenty minutes to make them soft and pliable. Then shake the casings so excess water falls off, and then place them momentarily on some paper toweling to drain.

Meanwhile, you can remove the cutting knife and grinding plate from your meat grinder and attach the casing stuffer spout. Also gather several yards of lightweight cotton string that you'll later need to tie off the casings in various locations.

The most common mistake made by first-time sausage makers is slipping one end of a casing over the end of the stuffing spout and then trying to fill the entire casing as it lays draped in coils on the tabletop. It just doesn't work because several big globs of the sausage mixture will clog the casing and go no farther. The correct method of stuffing sausage is to place one end of the casing over the mouth of the stuffer spout and push it as far back as possible.

Then continue pushing the remainder of the casing onto the spout until the entire four-foot-long casing is all scrunched up in accordion-like fashion. When you reach the other end of the casing, tie it closed with a bit of your string.

One person can stuff the casing himself, but a helper makes the job proceed much more quickly. One person turns the grinder's crank handle, or operates the on-off switch if it's an electric grinder, and simultaneously feeds the bulk sausage into the mouth or overhead hopper of the grinder. The helper works with the casings.

The first bulk sausage to come out of the grinder will fill up the little loose end of casing hanging from the stuffer spout. As the casing continues to fill and balloon out, additional casing material is slowly pulled off the spout and allowed to duly fill.

At this point, you've got two choices. You can slowly fill a two-foot-long segment of casing to make a so-called "ring," whereupon it's then tied off, or you can make shorter, six-inch-long sausage links which, individually, are not tied off. If you plan to later smoke the sausage, you'll want to make rings, as they are much easier to hang in a smokehouse or small electric smoker. If you'll be freezing the sausage with intentions of later frying, baking, or grilling it, links are easier to work with.

The way to segment your individual links is to first let six inches of casing fill, then momentarily turn off the grinder or cease turning the crank han-

As the casing begins to fill with sausage, occasionally twist the casing to form links, then pull a bit more casing off the end of the stuffing spout.

dle. Next, turn the sausage link two or three times to make a twist in the casing. It's important to remember to make successive twists always in the same direction; otherwise, if you were to make a right-hand twist in the first casing link, and then a left-hand twist in the second casing link, the second twisting, going in the opposite direction, will have a tendency to untwist the first. As previously mentioned, there's no need to make string ties between each link because the twists, as soon as the casing dries a bit, will remain securely in place; the only string ties needed are to close the ends of the first and final links.

One other little trick should be mentioned, and it's something that can be gained only through hands-on experience. You want to make sure your

127

When you've completed as many links as you want on a series of sausages, string-tie the end of the last link, cut the chain of sausages free, then begin making another chain as before.

casing is stuffed tightly and that small spaces or air pockets between clumps of sausage are eliminated. Otherwise, during later cooking, these will become tiny pressure cookers that will allow steam build-up to split the sausages. The trick, therefore, is to keep enough finger tension on the accordioned casing so it doesn't slide off the stuffing spout too easily, as this will invariably result in slack-filled links or rings. Yet at the same time you don't want to stuff your sausages so tightly that you risk rupturing the rather fragile casings and subsequently having sausage mixture spilling on your table. To obtain just the right shape and degree of compactness, using your fingertips to squeeze, mold, and shape the sausage links seems to be the most popular way of getting everything just right.

All of this may sound terribly complicated but after only ten minutes of trial and error you'll be producing sausages that look like they were created by an artist.

A Few Words on Smoking

A small, inexpensive smoker of the type designed for use by sportsmen for smoking fish and game is perfect. But realize you will not be achieving an internal sausage temperature sufficient to either eliminate the possibility of trichinosis from the pork or achieve necessary preservation attributes in order that the finished sausage does not need refrigeration.

Consequently, submitting sausage to the smoker for several hours should be looked upon only as a method of enhancing the flavor of the sausage, and it still needs to be cooked before being eaten. It also needs to be stored in your refrigerator, if it will be eaten within one week, or in your freezer if it's to be stored longer.

Authentic smoked sausage, which requires no refrigeration, such as some

Making bulk sausage begins with cutting pork, suet, and venison into chunks.

types of pepperoni and summer sausage, is treated in an entirely different manner. These are fully cooked, in bulk form, in vats of boiling water (or, sometimes they are allowed to soak and cure in a brine solution), then they are stuffed into casings, and after that smoked until an internal temperature of at least 110°F is achieved. Since there are so many techniques and fine points dealing with this aspect of sausage making, I suggest to obtain a book specifically on the subject of smoking meats.

An endless variation of sausage flavors can be achieved through a combination of the seasoning spices and the type of hardwood or fruitwood chips used during the smoking process. In all cases, the finished smoked sausage must be refrigerated or frozen for long-term storage.

14

Freezing and Defrosting Venison

I t's widely accepted among professionals in the food-handling industry that the quality of any type of meat taken out of a freezer is never any better than the quality that goes in. Unfortunately, some hunters seem to think that the freezing of their venison is a cure-all for poor handling practices in the field, at camp, in transit, or at the homefront.

I'm reminded of the time that I found a two-year-old rump roast in our freezer that had somehow gotten lost in the shuffle when subsequent deer had been taken. I just couldn't bring myself to throw out the roast, even though it had a bit of freezer burn around one edge. So I trimmed off the burn and, since I suspected in advance that the interior of the roast might be a bit dry, I chose a moist-cooking recipe. The meal was delectable.

Coincidentally, I was later describing this experience to a friend who had remarked that his own cache of freezer venison wasn't tasting very good of late, even though it was only four months old. I was shocked when I opened his freezer and saw a disarray of packages wrapped with only one layer of freezer paper and in some cases just one layer of plastic wrap. Some of the packages had part of the paper actually torn in places, which allowed portions of the meat to be exposed, and some of the packages didn't even have labels on them.

It would be difficult to entirely blame these atrocious storage methods for the venison tasting so badly–possibly, the deer wasn't cared for properly in the field, or was aged so long it reached the point of spoilage–but I'd bet my friend's careless wrapping of his venison was at least partly responsible.

Refrigerator Storage of Venison

Typically, a successful hunter places most of his venison in a freezer for later use. However, he's almost certain to want to serve several dinners to his family almost immediately. This meat can be stored, unfrozen, in his refrigerator for a brief period of time. Refer to the following guidelines for safe storage times of particular cuts or types of venison.

Refrigerator Storage

Refrigerator Temperature - 38° to 40°F

Steaks: 2 - 4 days
Roasts: 2 - 4 days
Tenderloins: 2 - 4 days
Deerburger: 1 - 2 days
Sausage: 3 - 7 days
Stew Meat: (chunks) 1 - 3 days
Leftover Cooked Meat: 4 - 5 days

Many food experts I've consulted with have said that how you store venison in your refrigerator is just as important as carefully heeding the length of its storage-time limitations. As strange as it sounds, fresh meat should be stored unwrapped because exposure to air facilitates a slight drying of the surface of the meat which, in turn, increases its keeping quality. It's advised, therefore, to place the meat on a plate and cover it loosely with a small towel that has been dampened and then wrung out. Or, wrap the meat loosely in brown or white butcher's paper. Although moisture- and vapor-proof materials such as freezer wrapping paper and clear plastic wraps are ideal for freezing and long-term storage of meat, they should not be used for limited refrigerator storage.

Incidentally, when you purchase meat–be it beef, pork or whatever–at your local grocery store, it's usually sitting on some type of foam tray and wrapped tightly with plastic that's been heat-sealed. Meat purchased this way can go right into your freezer. But, if you plan to eat it within several days, and store it in your refrigerator in the meantime, you should remove the tight plastic cling-wrap and then set it on a plate covered with a towel as described above.

If your refrigerator has a special drawer for the storage of fresh meat, by all means use it. This compartment is invariably situated at the very bottom of the 'fridge where the temperature averages several degrees colder. Also since it is enclosed, you're able to discourage the possibility of flavor-transfers between your venison and other foods, or vice versa.

Best Freezer Wrapping Materials

Appropriate freezer wrapping materials accomplish several things simultaneously. They protect the venison from bumps and bruises as the meat packages are stacked and arranged in the freezer; they lock in meat moisture and juices to ensure the venison remains tender; and, they block out dry, stale freezer air, which can cause rancidity and give meat an "off" flavor.

So if you consider the responsibilities entrusted to your choice of freezer wrapping materials, it's poor economy to buy cheap materials, or wrap the meat improperly. Why risk the quality of your venison and all the work that, to this point, has gone into caring for it?

One acceptable approach is to begin with some type of cling-wrap as your first means of protecting your venison. This might be a transparent plastic freezer wrap such as Saran or cellophane, or even heavy-duty aluminum foil.

In any case they all serve as nonporous vapor barriers, which can be pressed and formed around the irregular surfaces of any meat to hug it tightly. This eliminates pockets of air trapped against the meat and at the same time prevents moisture from being drawn out or sublimated, which is what gives it a dry, blah taste.

With a cling-wrap tightly in place around the meat, cover it a second time with a quality-grade freezer wrapping paper with a glossy plastic coating on one side. The glossy, plastic side always goes on the inside.

This paper is quite heavy, which is what protects the meat when it occasionally contacts other items in the freezer. The plastic coating, on the other hand, serves as still another vapor barrier to prevent dry, cold freezer air from working its way into wrapped packages and doing its dastardly deed. It's this second wrap that is primarily responsible for preventing freezer burn, in which the meat in places becomes entirely depleted of surface moisture, discolored, and then rancid.

Aside from the specific materials you may elect to use, there are two wrapping methods I highly recommend. They're called the "drugstore wrap" and the "butcher's wrap."

The drugstore wrap works best when your venison cuts are relatively small, flat, of uniform thickness, and basically rectangular or oval shaped, as in wrapping backstrap steaks, round steaks, stew meat, link or ring sausages, and bulk quantities of burger or sausage. First lay out a rectangular sheet of the wrapping paper, with the glossy plastic side up, and place your venison (already tightly enclosed in a cling-wrap such as aluminum foil or Saran) in the center. Bring up the top and bottom edges and, holding them together in the middle, crease and fold them several times to bring them down snug and flat against the top of the meat. Then take the two tail ends, one at a time, and fold them inward, creating triangular flaps which can then be tucked under and taped in place.

The butcher's wrap works best for larger cuts of venison that are round, oval and of irregular thickness, such as rolled roasts (made from the shoulder, neck, or rump), or odd-shaped pieces such as rib plates. Lay out a square sheet of freezer wrapping paper, glossy side up. Place the cling-wrapped meat in one corner, then begin rolling it diagonally across the paper toward the opposite corner, folding over the right and left sides as you go.

To make the drugstore wrap, secure the meat in some type of cling-wrap such as Saran or foil to make it air-tight, and then lay it in the center of a piece of plastic-coated paper.

Bring up the two sides of the paper and fold over the opposing edges.

Crease and fold over the paper as many times as necessary until it lies tight and flat against the package.

134

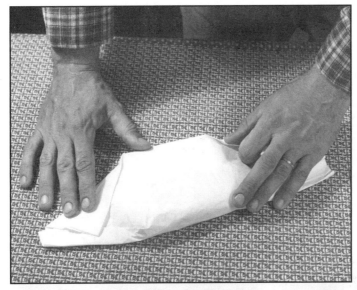

Fold the corners inward, then seal with tape and label.

To make the butcher's wrap, secure the venison in a cling-wrap or foil, then place the cut of meat in one corner of a sheet of plastic-coated paper.

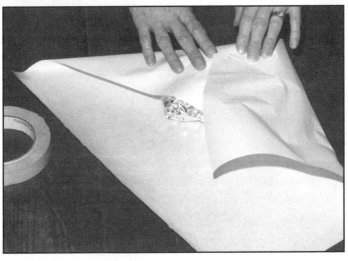

Tightly fold inward the right and left corners of the paper.

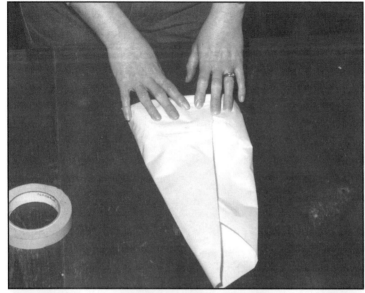

Make sure the paper is as tight as possible as you roll the meat diagonally toward the opposite corner of the paper.

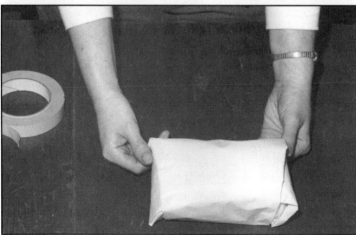

This is the completed butcher's wrap. Again, use tape to seal the edges, then label the package as to contents, weight, and date frozen.

When your wrapping is completed, use tape to seal any edges or seams. One word of caution. Don't use cellophane tape, as it will loosen when subjected to the cold air of your freezer. Common masking tape found in any store's hardware department is recommended; the very same tape, found in a store's houseware department, is called "freezer tape," at double the price.

Labeling is a very important part of freezing venison because you'll want to be able to identify various cuts of meat, their sizes, and when they were frozen. I recommend using a common laundry pen that contains indelible ink, which won't smear or fade when the paper wrapping material accumulates frost particles.

Freezing Your Venison

Everyone has some type of combination refrigerator/freezer in the kitchen but these are poor choices for long-term storage of meats.

Flash-freezing, sometimes also called sharp-freezing, which will be discussed in detail in a moment, ideally requires a temperature range between 10°F to 20°F and according to the United States Department of Agriculture (USDA), long-term storage of meat requires an internal freezer temperature that does not exceed 0°F.

Now here's the point to be made. Virtually all freezer units built in conjunction with refrigerators, especially the new energy-efficient and self-defrosting models, are incapable of achieving or sustaining internal temperatures lower than 15°F.

Consequently, these types of freezers are fine for storing vegetables, convenience foods, ice cream, and yes, even meats, provided the storage time of these foods is not allowed to exceed a few months. If you instead stack one of these freezers to the brim with several dozen packages of venison, and don't get around to defrosting and eating many of them for six months or longer, you'll undoubtedly experience a very sad and displeasing reunion with your deer.

For this reason, serious sportsmen, especially those who often find themselves in possession of large quantities of fish and game, also have a second freezer specifically for that purpose alone, and it may be either an upright model with shelves or a "low boy" chest-type freezer. Both types are easily capable of flash-freezing meats–freezing them as quickly as possible–and then maintaining them in near-perfect condition for long periods at subzero temperatures.

All meat has a high water content; when the meat freezes, the water also freezes, causing ice crystals. The slower you freeze meat, the larger these ice crystals are and thus the greater amount of cellular damage they are able to cause through expansion, which often results in the meat acquiring a mushy texture. Conversely, the faster meat is frozen, the smaller the ice crystals and, hence, the minimum amount of tissue damage.

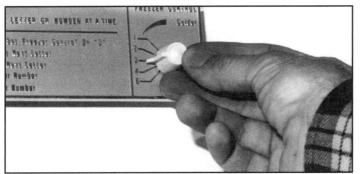

Before adding venison packages to your freezer, pre-condition it by turning its thermostat dial down to the lowest setting.

137

It stands to reason you can flash-freeze meat far more quickly if you have very cold meat to start with. So place your wrapped packages of venison inside your refrigerator for several hours to thoroughly chill them; if the available refrigerator space is limited, and it's bitter cold outside, place your venison packages in a cardboard box or camping cooler on the back porch for a few hours.

Meanwhile, turn the temperature dial of your freezer down to its coldest setting to properly "condition" the inside of the unit for flash-freezing.

Depending upon many variables, this conditioning period may take as long as two hours or as little as thirty minutes. A small thermometer is a wise investment as it tells you when the internal temperature is at least 10°F and, therefore, conducive to flash-freezing.

You can now begin transferring your wrapped venison packages to the freezer, but don't put them all in at once because this will tend to raise the internal temperature and overload the freezer's flash-freezing capability. Place only one-third of the venison packages in the freezer, then wait two hours before adding another one-third, and so on, never adding more than thirty-pounds of meat at a time.

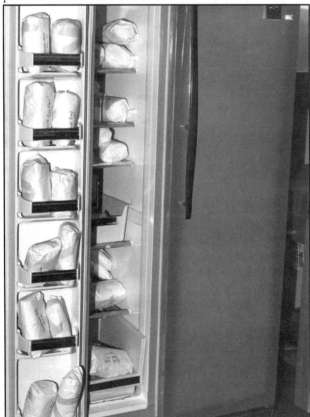

Both chest and upright freezers are fine for long-term storage of venison. Just be sure to add only one-third of your wrapped venison packages at a time, so the freezer's internal temperature is not drastically raised. Meanwhile, store the remaining packages in your refrigerator to keep them cold.

When placing your meat packages in the freezer, position them as close as possible to the freezer's walls, where the coils are located, and make sure they do not come in direct contact with each other, as that would retard freezing air from circulating around and between them. As each one-third of the venison packages is frozen solidly, it can moved toward the center of the freezer, with the next load then going directly against the walls.

The following day, when all of the venison packages are frozen rock solid, you can then arrange or stack them any way you please. At that time, also be sure to return the freezer's temperature dial to its original setting, checking your thermometer a day later to ensure the freezer is maintaining an internal temperature of no higher than 0°F.

Freezer Storage Time

Freezer temperature - 0°F

Large roasts: 12 - 14 months
Small roasts: 8 - 10 months
Large, barded roasts: 6 - 8 months
Small, barded roasts: 5 - 6 months
Steaks (round, sirloin tip): 8 - 10 months
Steaks (backstrap, tenderloin): 6 - 8 months
Stew meat: 6 - 8 months
Burger: 6 - 8 months
Sausage: 3 - 4 months
Leftover cooked meat: 2 - 3 months

Vacuum Packing

The premier meat-wrapping and freezing method is vacuum packing, which entirely does away with wrapping-paper supplies and instead uses air-tight plastic bags.

Several years ago I invested in the FoodSaver, made by Tilia, Inc., which is the so-called Cadillac of all vacuum-packaging models on the market. It is so superior in the results it achieves that I've never looked back, never bought freezer wrapping paper again or, in fact, used any other freezing

The best freezer storage method of all is vacuum-sealing. Increasingly, hunting families are investing in these machines because their venison will remain frozen in perfect condition for up to three years. Plus, the machine can be used year-round for freezer-storage of all other types of meats and vegetables.

method for fish and game, domestic meats, vegetables, and fruits.

Essentially, here's how the system works. Taking a continuous roll of plastic-bag material, cut individual bags to length in accordance with the sizes of various food items to be frozen. One end of the bag is then placed under the machine's lid and you push a button; this step heat-seals that edge of the bag.

Next, the food item is placed in the opposite, still-open end of the newly created bag, and then that edge is placed in the machine. When you push another button, the machine sucks every bit of air out of the bag, causing the plastic to forcibly collapse around the food item's every contour, and then that edge is automatically sealed.

Since there is no oxygen remaining in the bag, and the food item is literally sealed in a vacuum, there is no way for ice crystals to form on the surface and the meat is preserved for a far longer period of time in one's freezer. How long? Studies by the University of California Department of Food Science and Technology have verified that meat items that are vacuum sealed have a freezer storage life of up to three years! And from first-hand experience I'll take an oath this is true.

In addition to freezing assorted cuts of venison, you also can freeze prepared meals and liquid items for the same length of time. This would include such items as stews made in large quantities, venison casseroles, and of course all manner of domestic meats, fruits, and vegetables that one can occasionally buy in large quantities at sale prices.

How to Defrost Venison

Many people have fallen into bad habits when it comes to defrosting meats. Too tired and stressed after a long day, they grab a meat package from the freezer and hold it under a stream of warm tap water to defrost it. Or they simply zap it on their microwave's defrost cycle.

Or, at the opposite extreme, they take the meat out of the freezer at breakfast time and let it sit on a sink drainboard all day, which allows the meat to come to room temperature and just sit there, soaking in its own accumulated juices, for another six hours.

Luckily, they get away with these abhorrent practices because domesticated livestock meats are so excessively treated with chemical additives that you can abuse them to no end and expect them to be at least marginally edible.

Venison suffers greatly when mishandled in such ways. To properly defrost venison, simply think about what kind of meal you'd like to have the following day and take an appropriate package of venison from the freezer the night before. But do not let it sit out and defrost at room temperature! Instead, place it in your refrigerator overnight. This way, it will remain very cold as it slowly defrosts and it will suffer no deterioration whatever.

One critical step that many people overlook is to unwrap the venison

Never defrost venison by letting it sit on a drainboard at room temperature. Defrost it overnight in your refrigerator, after first removing the wrapping material and setting the meat in a colander so juices and meltwater will drain away.

before placing it in the refrigerator to defrost overnight. After unwrapping, place the raw, still-frozen meat in a colander seated over a pan. Finally, dampen a small towel, wring it out thoroughly, and drape it over the meat. This prevents the meat, during defrosting, from soaking in the various fluids and juices that result from the ice crystals melting. If the meat is kept in a tightly enclosed wrapping, and the juices are not allowed to escape and drain away, the meat is likely to have a stale, unpleasant taste.

Also keep in mind that no meat should be allowed to completely defrost and then be refrozen in its existing state. The key word here is "defrost," because meat that is still extremely cold, rigid, and has visible ice crystals on its surface is not considered thawed. If need be, it can be returned to the freezer with no harm done at this stage.

However, completely thawed venison that is fully cooked can indeed be refrozen. In this case the key word is "cooked," because cooking so radically transforms the cellular structure of the meat that it's like starting all over with fresh food.

So, for example, if you defrost deerburger and use it to prepare spaghetti sauce for a meal, it's perfectly safe and acceptable to freeze leftover sauce for future use. Similarly, if you have a rump roast for dinner, any of the leftover, cooked meat can be frozen and defrosted at some later date for use in making a stew or casserole.

15

Meat-Tenderizing Techniques

We've all learned how our senses can fool us. The most common examples are with magic tricks and Hollywood special effects. When it comes to food, venison is one of the most deceptive of all meats and, as a result, every year it causes many well-intentioned cooks to ruin meals.

Simply put, venison, in its raw state, looks almost identical to beef. Consequently, many people make the mistake of trying to cook it as beef, and afterwards they expect it to taste like beef! In trying to cook their venison as they would beef, the results are often devastating. The texture of the meat not only turns out tough, but when it doesn't taste like beef, an

Experienced hunters know that beef and venison look identical, but that cooking them the same way is disastrous! Don't become a victim of sensory deception.

alarm bell rings. They curl their lips and begin suspecting the meat is spoiled. Or they comment about it being "wild and gamy."

Actually, all that has happened, as with any talented magician performing sleight of hand, is that they've become honest, innocent victims of their own preconceived ideas and sensory deception.

Characteristics of Venison

There are only two things venison and beef have in common. Both are red meats and both provide good eating. Other than that, few similarities exist. Tatoo that on your forehead so that it's always at the forefront of your consciousness to dictate your approach to handling, cooking, and serving deer meat.

One of the major differences between venison and beef is fat content, which influences the flavors and textures of the two meats and therefore how you cook them and how they subsequently taste.

Overall, the tissue structure of beef is relatively fine grained and marbled. Conversely, venison is more coarsely grained, very lean (possessing minimal marbling) and, due to the diets of deer, just a bit tangy and robust.

I know certain individuals, dedicated woodsmen, who raised their children on wild game. And when the kids eventually tasted beefsteak for the first time, not until their adolescent years, they thought something was wrong with it. They claimed it was soft and mushy and had no flavor. They were simply victims of sensory deception, only this time in reverse.

As a result of the high fat content in beef, it can be cooked far longer than venison and still be tender. Venison is a lean, dry meat to begin with, with very little in the way of internal basting or lubricating fat to seep throughout the tissue fibers and subsequently break them down. Not only that, but by the time a deer is one and one-half years old, its musculature has long since hardened off—that is, individual tissue fibers have greatly com-

Compared to beef, venison is very lean and dry. It lacks the internal marbling that tenderizes beef, so hunters must use substitute measures to make up for the difference.

pacted themselves. And in cooking any type of meat, it's typically the long tissue fibers that prove to be the most tender when cooked; with meat possessing short tissue fibers, it's easy to quickly cook it beyond the point of no return in terms of tenderness.

One remedy that helps to tenderize deer meat is proper aging (see Chapter 7). Fat can also be added to the venison through the techniques of larding and barding (see Chapter 10). Let's look at two other interim procedures that can be enacted upon your venison before it makes its journey to your stove or oven.

The Wonderful World of Marinades

What makes meat tender? As noted, interstitial marbling is important, but is not the entire explanation; an even greater role is played by the twenty-five different categories of enzymes found in all types of meats.

Enzymes are chemical ferments that, through a process known as oxidation, work on proteins, carbohydrates, and fats in meats to break down the connective tissue, reducing it to a gelatinous consistency. This process not only makes meat tender but also enhances its flavor and juiciness through the release of water held in the meat.

Because of differences in their chemical constitution and the related activity of enzymes, animal fats vary considerably in their tendency to oxidize. Pork fat, for example, oxidizes much faster than beef fat; hence, the enzymatic breakdown of connective tissue is more complete, and this is why a pork roast with a marbling content comparable to a similar-size beef roast will always be far more tender than the beef.

Venison fat, on the other hand, oxidizes slowly and, aggravating the situation, there is not much interstitial fat (marbling) to begin with. Consequently, if cooked like pork or beef, venison can be as tough to chew as an old truck tire. This is why, in larding or barding venison, I recommended the use of bacon, salt pork, beef fat, or beef suet.

In the absence of these pork-fat or beef-fat additives, you can take a chemical approach to tenderizing venison if you suspect the deer is old and past its prime. But don't let the word "chemical" freak you out because, in this context, I'm not referring to synthetic compounds created in a laboratory but, rather, a blending

Preparing a marinade to soak venison in before cooking is a splendid way to tenderize the meat. With some marinade recipes, the venison flavor can be enhanced to give the meat a tangy flavor.

of fully natural ingredients into a marinade.

A marinade is a liquid bath in which otherwise tougher cuts of venison are allowed to soak for various lengths of time before being cooked. Shoulder roasts (that is, arm and blade roasts), neck roasts, and in the case of very old deer the sirloin tip roasts, are the ones most frequently given a marinating treatment.

There are literally hundreds of popular marinade recipes to choose from, but all share the common bond of possessing some type of highly acidic or enzymatic ingredient such as vinegar, wine, salt brine, whole milk, buttermilk, or baking soda. All of these greatly accelerate the otherwise slow enzymatic oxidation process that breaks down a meat's connective tissue and makes it tender.

The dozens of combinations of remaining ingredients commonly found in marinades simply add their own flavors to the venison. The two exceptions to this rule are milk and baking soda marinades, which do not impart any flavors whatsoever. This is a terrific situation for the hunter planning to marinate some cut of venison. He can enhance the flavor of the venison with any number of potions. Or, he can accomplish the same goals of marinating and all the while retain the exclusive flavor of the venison with nothing competing or detracting from its uniqueness. Following are the marinade recipes I rely upon most.

Marinade # 1

1-½ cups vinegar	1 teaspoon dried thyme
¾ cup vegetable oil	1 teaspoon black pepper
2 cups water	2 cloves
3 slices onion	1 large bay leaf
1 carrot, diced	1 tablespoon salt
2 garlic cloves, crushed	

In a large saucepan, bring all of the ingredients to a boil while stirring continually, then reduce the heat and simmer for fifteen minutes. Turn the heat off and allow the marinade to cool. Meanwhile, use an ice pick to randomly punch holes in the venison roast. Place the roast in a glass or plastic bowl (never use a metal bowl with a marinade), pour the marinade over the top of the meat until it is entirely covered, cover the bowl, then place it in your refrigerator for twenty-four hours. Turn the meat once every six or eight hours. The following day, remove the roast, pat dry with paper toweling, then use your favorite cooking recipe.

Marinade # 2

2 cups dry red wine	1 carrot, diced
¼ cup vinegar	½ teaspoon black pepper
1 cup water	1 bay leaf, broken
½ cup vegetable oil	2 stalks celery, chopped
1 small onion, chopped	1 tablespoon parsley flakes

Mix all of the ingredients thoroughly, pour over the venison in a glass or plastic bowl, cover with a lid, then refrigerate for twenty-four hours, turning the meat frequently.

Marinade # 3

1 quart cold water	3 tablespoons vinegar
3 tablespoons salt	

Thoroughly mix the ingredients, then pour over venison in a bowl and soak in your refrigerator overnight. The next day, remove the venison from the marinade and rinse thoroughly under cold tap water before proceeding with your favorite recipe.

Marinade #3 is a basic brine marinade that should be discarded after use. However, Marinades #1 and #2 can be stored in a glass jar in your refrigerator for up to three months and reused whenever you like.

Also, it's perfectly acceptable to vary the first two marinade recipes in accordance with your own tastes. For example, in place of the dry red wine in Marinade #2, you can add white wine or a robust burgundy.

Other common marinade ingredients that can be added to, or substituted for, other ingredients in Marinades #1 and #2 include a splash of lemon juice, diced green pepper, ginger, soy sauce, sugar, orange juice, allspice, tarragon, rosemary, Worcestershire sauce, beer (light or dark), or a touch of bourbon. Feel free to experiment and you're certain to discover specific marinade flavors you like better than others.

As mentioned earlier, there are two marinades that impart no flavors of their own. Both are simple to make. One is the baking soda marinade, prepared by mixing one quart of cold water, one-half cup baking soda, and one teaspoon salt. Blend the ingredients until the soda and salt are dissolved, then pour the liquid over the meat in the usual way and place in your refrigerator overnight. Rinse the meat before using any recipe.

If you want to use a marinade to tenderize venison without additional enhancement, plain buttermilk is the choice.

To use milk as a marinade (buttermilk is preferred to whole milk, but both are suitable with no residual flavors imparted to the venison), simply place the meat in a bowl, cover with the milk, refrigerate overnight; then rinse the meat before using.

You can also buy bottled, commercially made marinades in most grocery stores. They're found in the salad dressing section, and the most common brand is Lawry's. The company makes some intriguing marinade flavors that are splendid not only with venison but with gamebirds and waterfowl as well; they include Mesquite, Hawaiian Tropical Fruit, Herb and Garlic, Dijon and Honey, Hickory and Apple Cider, Tequila Lime, Thai Ginger, Caribbean Jerk, Teriyaki and Pineapple Juice, and Mediterranean.

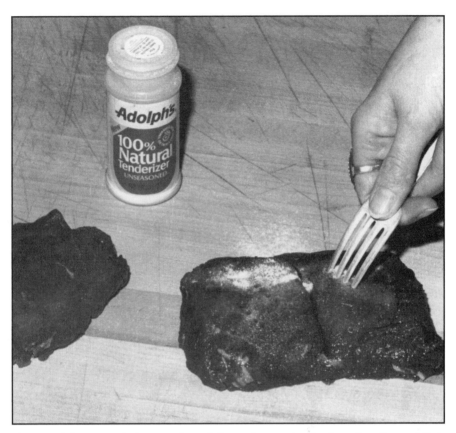

Commercial meat tenderizers work much faster than marinades, impart no flavor of their own, and are ideal for thinner cuts of venison such as steaks.

Meat–Tenderizing Salts

In addition to marinades for tenderizing venison, commercial meat tenderizers, which are available in all grocery stores, do a splendid job. With these, you gain the advantage of being able to begin cooking almost immediately because there is no delayed soaking period as with marinades.

These tenderizers are saltlike, crystalline compounds made entirely from natural ingredients and contain active enzymes that attack a meat's connective tissue and break it down. Adolph's Meat Tenderizer is perhaps the most widely recognized brand name and its active ingredient is a vegetable enzyme called "papain," obtained from the papaya melon. Other companies use bromelin, an extract from the pineapple, and ficin enzymes, from various tropical flowers, with equally good results.

Regardless of the particular brand name you elect to use, for the enzymatic action to occur efficiently it is important to sprinkle the tenderizer evenly over all sides of the meat at a rate of one teaspoon per pound. Then the meat should be pierced deeply with a fork. There's no waiting period; begin immediately with your favorite recipe.

Finally, here's a special trick very few know about. If you'd like to enhance the flavor of venison by using a marinade, but you don't have time to allow the meat to sit in your refrigerator overnight, do this: add two tablespoons of meat tenderizer to each cup of prepared marinade, mix thoroughly, pour over the meat, and you can cut your marinating time down to two hours.

16

Steaks, Chops, and Roasts
to Brag About

E very serious hunter should have a collection of wild game cookbooks. I've written five myself and have more than forty others
in my kitchen library that I regularly consult. Understandably,
I've experimented with, refined, and even created hundreds of
venison recipes over the years. One interesting thing I've learned
is that it's more often the cooking method, not the particular selection of
ingredients, that determines the outcome.

In the remaining chapters, where I describe many long-time favorite
recipes, I'll first describe cooking methods for various cuts of venison, with

Serious hunters
who take at least
one deer every
year, plus assorted
other species,
should have a
library of game
cookbooks. This is
Jackie Bushman,
founder of
Buckmasters.

Roasts such as rolled shoulder roasts should be cooked only until medium-rare with a blush of pink in the middle. Cook beyond this point, and the venison steadily becomes tougher.

the actual recipes that follow being of less importance to the outcome. That way, no matter which recipe is selected, the meat should turn out tender, flavorful, and delicious.

Roasting is a technique in which a venison roast is placed (fat-side up if draped with bacon or other fat) on a rack in an open, shallow roasting pan. The rack holds the roast out of the grease, and the bacon or other fat dribbles down slowly and bastes the roast as it cooks.

In such cooking, it is imperative that a meat thermometer be used to monitor the progress of the roast. Insert the thermometer so the bulb is in the center of the thickest part of the meat, and make sure that the bulb does not touch bone or the bottom of the pan. A venison roast should be cooked only until it is medium-rare to medium on the inside, with a blush of juicy bright pink to the meat's color. Forget that you may like your beef roasts well done. Venison is not beef!

If you look at your meat thermometer, you'll see a graduated temperature scale paired to the desired "doneness" of various types of meat such as beef, pork, and fowl. Venison won't be listed on the scale, meaning that you have to go by temperature alone, and to achieve a roast that is medium-rare to medium you should cook it until its internal temperature registers 140° to 150°F (by comparison, a well-done beef roast has an internal temperature of 160° to 170°F).

Ideally, your roasting pan should sit on the middle shelf-rack in your oven, and the temperature dial of the oven should be set at 300° to 350°F, depending upon the size of the roast. Very large roasts (more than six pounds) should be cooked at the lower temperature and mid-size roasts (two to five

When broiling, as with sirloin tip steaks, whether over coals or under the oven's broiler, use high heat to briefly sear both sides, never allowing the inside to go beyond medium-rare.

pounds) at the higher temperature. You should never use a dry-heat cooking method with roasts smaller than two pounds because they will turn out tough and dry, so always use a roast of ample size; if it's larger than what your family can consume at one meal, the leftovers can be served in sandwiches, soups, or stews.

Broiling is another dry-heat cooking method, but this technique is generally reserved for tenderloin steaks, backstrap steaks, or sirloin tip steaks. Steaks to be broiled should be at least three-quarter-inch thick, but not more than one and one-half inches thick. Turn your oven's regulator dial to broil, or to its highest setting (generally, 500°F), and remember that the oven door should be left slightly ajar.

Place your venison steaks on the rack of your broiler pan so the juices can drain away (otherwise, they may flame up) and situate the pan so the meat will be from two to five inches from the heat source. Here is where each cook will have to temper his decisions with good judgment because the heat output of gas broilers, compared to electric, can vary quite a bit; also,

Pan-broiling (or pan-frying), which can also be done on a griddle, is best reserved for sirloin tip or backstrap steaks. Sprinkle just a bit of salt on the cooking surface and you can reduce the amount of cooking oil by half.

thicker steaks should be placed farther away from the heat than thin ones.

Broil the steaks just until their top sides begin to brown, then flip them and broil on the other side for about one-half the previously allotted time. You may wish to barely slice into one of the steaks to check its progress. Those who broil beef steaks claim this heresy, that cutting into them will allow their juices to escape. True, but in the case of venison this small loss is better than relying purely upon guesswork and perchance allowing the steaks to broil just one minute too long and become overdone.

I advise against cooking a venison steak beyond the point of medium-rare, as this stage is when it's at its best. In cooking outdoors over a propane or charcoal grill, simply use the same method as with beef steaks but, again, never permit the meat to cook beyond medium-rare.

Pan-broiling is a splendid method of cooking steaks, but few people are familiar with it. A heavy, cast-iron skillet or griddle is necessary; it should be sparingly brushed with just a bit of cooking oil. One-half teaspoon of oil should be plenty to prevent the meat from sticking; if you add more than this you are no longer pan-broiling but panfrying.

Lay your steaks in the pan and then cook them over very low heat. Since the meat is in direct contact with the skillet or griddle, it is essential to turn the meat occasionally to ensure even cooking. The steaks are ready to serve when they are slightly brown on both sides and pink and juicy in the middle.

Panfrying is similar to pan-broiling in that a heavy skillet or griddle is used. However, substantially more cooking oil is used and the meat is cooked at a much higher temperature. While pan-broiling is ideally suited to thick steaks, panfrying is best accomplished with thinner steaks that have been floured or breaded.

Panfrying typically results in the outer surfaces and edges of steaks achieving just a bit of crispness, which, depending upon the recipe ingredients in the breading, enhances the flavor of the meat. In achieving this desirable

The tenderloins and backstraps are also perfectly suited to being cubed and then grilled or broiled as shish-kabobs.

result, there may be some sacrifice of tenderness. So, beforehand, you may desire to treat your meat (especially sirloin tip steaks) to a dose of commercially prepared meat tenderizer.

One thing to guard against in panfrying is a burner temperature that becomes so hot your fat or grease begins to smoke. Another axiom of panfrying is to turn the meat frequently to ensure even cooking but, still again, venison steaks should never be cooked beyond medium.

Finally, one trick that ensures success, no matter which cooking method you decide to use, is that your intended serving platter and dinner plates be preheated. I like to simply slip them into the oven for five minutes before the meal is served.

The necessity of hot dinnerware has to do with the fat content in venison compared to beef. Remember that beef has a good deal of interstitial fat, or marbling, which gets extremely hot during cooking and therefore helps to retain the temperature of the meat long afterwards. Because venison does not have much fat woven between its tissue fibers, it cools quickly.

As a result, if you remove a venison roast from the oven, or steaks from the broiler or skillet, and place the meat on a cold platter straight from the cupboard, and then those seated transfer meat from the platter to their cold dinner plates, you're in for an unpleasant experience. Before anyone is even half finished eating they'll begin remarking upon how their venison is becoming colder and tougher with each bite. A hot serving platter and pre-heated dinner plates are the answer.

Now let's look at a number of recipes that call for roasting, broiling, pan-broiling, or panfrying the tender cuts of venison. Keep in mind that you can vary any of the following recipes, especially those calling for roasts, by first soaking your venison in a marinade.

Sauteed Steaks or Chops

¼ cup butter (½ stick)
1 teaspoon Lawry's Seasoned Salt
4 inch-thick steaks or chops

Melt the butter in a skillet, then blend in one teaspoon of the seasoned salt. Place the steaks in the pan and cook them slowly over medium heat until they are browned on all sides and pink and juicy in the middle. Serves four.

Spicy Deer Steaks Marinade

flour
3 tablespoons butter
3 tablespoons cooking oil
4 inch-thick steaks or chops

Use a marinade that contains wine, vegetable juice, or citrus juice, pour it over the steaks in a bowl, and refrigerate overnight. Drain and pat dry with paper towels. Flour the steaks well, then panfry in a skillet over medium heat containing the butter and cooking oil. Serves four.

Georgia-Style Steaks

4 steaks or chops
1 cup ketchup
1 tablespoon salt
1 tablespoon chili powder
2 tablespoons tarragon
1 onion, chopped
⅓ cup A-1 Steak Sauce

In a skillet, sear the steaks in just a bit of cooking oil on medium-high heat. Meanwhile, in a saucepan, bring all the remaining ingredients to a boil, stirring continually. Transfer the steaks to a shallow roasting pan, pour the sauce over the top and bake for one and one-half hours at 350°F. Serves four.

Venison Teriyaki

2 pounds tenderloin steak
3 tablespoons olive oil
3 tablespoons soy sauce
½ teaspoon garlic powder
1 tablespoon lemon juice
1 tablespoon brown sugar
2 cups uncooked Minute Rice
1 green bell pepper, sliced into strips
1 sweet white onion, sliced
1 cup sliced mushrooms
1 cup beef broth or bouillon

Slice the tenderloin into thin strips. Add the olive oil and soy sauce to a wok or high-sided skillet, then stir in the garlic, lemon juice, and brown sugar. Heat the wok or skillet on medium-high heat until the liquid begins to steam. Add the tenderloin strips and stir-fry them until they are almost cooked. Meanwhile, prepare the Minute Rice according to the package instructions. Now add to the wok or skillet the green pepper, onion, mushrooms, and broth. Turn the heat down to medium, cover, and slowly cook until everything is steaming. Ladle over a bed of the rice. Serves four.

High-Country Buttermilk Venison

4 backstrap or sirloin tip steaks
1 cup buttermilk
cooking oil
flour

Cut the steaks into one-inch cubes, then pound each with a meat hammer to about one-half-inch thick. Place the meat in a bowl, cover with the buttermilk, and allow the steak to soak for two hours. Then dredge the pieces in flour and panfry. Serves four.

Pepper Steak

4 backstrap or sirloin tip steaks
black pepper
2 tablespoons butter
2 tablespoons olive oil
4 teaspoons brandy

Sprinkle a bit of the pepper on both sides of the steaks and then gently pound it into the meat with a meat hammer. Add the butter and olive oil to a skillet and quickly sear the steaks on both sides. Turn the heat down to low and continue cooking until they are medium-rare. Meanwhile, warm the brandy in a small saucepan. When the steaks are ready, transfer them to a preheated platter. At tableside, pour the brandy over the steaks and ignite it. It will briefly flare up and then burn out. Serves four.

Kate's Venison Cutlets

2 pounds steak meat, 1/4-inch thick
1 cup seasoned (salt & pepper) flour
2 eggs
1-1/2 cups milk
1 cup Italian-seasoned bread crumbs
1/4 cup Parmesan cheese
1 teaspoon garlic powder
olive oil
1 - 10-ounce can whole, cooked asparagus
1/2 pound crisp bacon, crumble
1/2 pound sliced Swiss cheese

Preheat oven to 400°F. Dredge the cutlets in the seasoned flour. Dip each into a bowl of blended eggs and milk, then coat with a mixture of the bread crumbs, Parmesan cheese, and garlic powder. Heat one-half inch of olive oil in a skillet and fry the cutlets for one minute on each side. Transfer to paper toweling to briefly drain. Place on a cookie sheet. Place two whole asparagus spears on each cutlet, top with bacon bits and one slice of Swiss cheese. Place in the oven until the cheese melts. Serves six.

–Kate Fiduccia

Cracker-Fried Steaks

4 backstrap or sirloin tip steaks
2 eggs, beaten
1 cup saltine crackers, finely crushed
cooking oil

Dip each steak into the beaten egg, roll in the cracker crumbs, then pound gently with a meat hammer. Dip the steaks a second time in the egg, then roll again in the cracker crumbs. Fry in the cooking oil until the cracker coating has a toastlike color and appearance, no more! Serves four.

Sirloin Tip Roast

1 - 2 ½-pound sirloin tip roast
2 cloves garlic, slivered
2 tablespoons Dijon-style mustard
1 tablespoon chopped fresh thyme
½ teaspoon black pepper

Preheat oven to 325°F. Using the tip of a knife, cut small, evenly spaced slits in the roast and insert the garlic slivers. Rub the roast with the mustard, then sprinkle with the thyme and pepper. Place on a roasting pan, then place in the oven until the temperature reads 140° to 145°F. Transfer to a warm serving platter, remove the string ties, and slice thinly. Serves six.

Iron Range Venison Roast

1 3-pound rolled rump or shoulder roast
1 teaspoon fennel seed
1 teaspoon sage
1 teaspoon sugar
1 teaspoon salt
½ teaspoon black pepper

Carefully remove the string ties so you can open the roast. Spread the venison out as much as possible and make numerous scoring cuts across the meat with a knife. In a bowl, blend all the remaining ingredients, then sprinkle evenly over the meat. Roll the meat back up into its original shape and make new string ties. Insert a meat thermometer, drape the roast with bacon, and set in a roasting pan. Roast at 325°F until the internal temperature registers 145°F. Serves six.

Steak Sandwiches

1-½ pounds loin steak meat
cooking oil
1 green bell pepper, sliced
1 sweet white onion, sliced

Slice the tenderloin or backstrap meat thinly, then briefly sear in a frying pan containing a small amount of hot oil. Add the pepper and onion slices, cover, and continue cooking over low heat until the vegetables are cooked but still crisp. Toss briefly and then serve on hard-crusted sandwich rolls or warmed tortilla-fajita wraps. Serves four.

17

Terrific Pot Roasts and Braised Venison

W hile the dry-heat cooking methods described in the last chapter are designed chiefly for very tender cuts of venison, moist-heat cooking methods work best for not-so-tender cuts that need a bit of help if they are to provide toothsome fare.

We're referring here to venison cuts from the front legs, such as rolled shoulder roasts, blade roasts, and arm roasts. But we can also include rolled roasts from the neck, and even venison from the otherwise tender rear legs but when taken from an old, grizzled buck that is likely to be on the tough side.

These meals traditionally are done in a pot or deep pan on top of the stove, in the oven, or even in a vessel such as a Crockpot. In any of these cases, the idea is to cook the meat in a closed environment so that steam is trapped and softens the meat's connective tissue. The steam comes from a small amount of liquid added to the cooking vessel in accordance with the

Virtually any cut of venison from the front or back legs, or from the backstraps, is suitable for braising. These are backstrap steaks that have been cooked to tender perfection.

As a rule, pot roasts usually are first browned over high heat in a skillet.

particular recipe you're following. Generally the liquid is water, vegetable juice, soup, or wine.

What I especially like about cooking pot roasts or using a braising recipe is that you can often put potatoes, vegetables, and other items right in with the meat, which vastly simplifies meal preparation. And, depending upon the recipe, you frequently obtain a rich, sumptuous gravy as a special bonus. Still other times, only vegetables are added to the meat while it cooks, and the mixture is then served over a bed of potatoes, rice, or noodles.

The pot roast is then transferred to a pot along with seasonings and the other ingredients a recipe may call for.

The pot is then covered and tranferred to a pre-heated oven, or it can slow-cook on a stovetop burner.

The beauty of pot roasts is that you can throw potatoes and other vegetables right in with the meat to produce a one-pot meal. This one is being prepared in a cast-iron Dutch oven over campfire coals.

Five-Minute Pot Roast

1 2-pound shoulder or neck roast
1 cup water
1 envelope dry onion soup mix

This is the fastest, easiest pot roast I know of and, happily, one of the most delicious. Place your roast in the center of a square sheet of heavy-duty aluminum foil and bring the edges up and around the sides to form a pouch. Pour one cup of water over the top of the roast, then sprinkle on the dry soup mix. Now pinch together the edges of the foil to form a tight seal to trap steam, and place the pouch in a shallow roasting pan. Place in a 325°F oven for one and one-half hours. When you open the pouch to slice the meat you'll find it tender beyond belief and, as a special surprise, you'll have a good quantity of perfect gravy you can ladle over noodles or potatoes. As with all venison, remember to serve on a hot platter. Serves four.

German Pot Roast

1 3-pound shoulder or neck roast
2 onions, chopped
1 teaspoon garlic powder
4 tablespoons butter
¼ cup vinegar
1 cup tomato sauce
½ teaspoon poultry seasoning
¼ teaspoon nutmeg
¼ teaspoon cinnamon
¼ teaspoon allspice

In a skillet, saute the onions with the garlic powder in the butter, then transfer to a plate where they will stay hot. In the same skillet, sear the roast until it is brown on all sides. Transfer the meat to an oven-proof pot, spoon the onions over the top, pour the vinegar and tomato sauce into the pot, then sprinkle the seasonings on top of the meat. Cover the pot with a lid and cook slowly in a 300°F oven for two hours. After placing the meat on a hot platter and slicing it, pour the juices from the pot over the meat. Serves four (with leftovers for sandwiches the next day).

Pot Roast Elegante

1 2-pound shoulder or neck roast
salt and pepper
1 medium can condensed cream soup
1 onion, sliced

In a skillet, brown the roast on all sides in a bit of cooking oil. Transfer the roast to a pot or oven-tempered glass casserole dish and sprinkle with a bit of salt and pepper. Pour on top of the roast and around the sides a can of condensed soup (cream of mushroom, cream of celery, or some other favorite). Lay the onion slices on top, cover, and slow-cook at 325°F for one and one-half hours. Transfer the roast to a hot platter, slice, then pour the cream gravy from the cooking pot over the top. Serves four.

Pot Roast Italiano

1 2-pound shoulder or neck roast
1 medium can condensed cream soup
½ cup dry red wine
2 tablespoons parsley flakes
½ teaspoon thyme
1 bay leaf, crumbled
salt and pepper

In a skillet, brown the roast on all sides in cooking oil. Transfer the roast to a pot or oven-tempered casserole dish. In a bowl, blend the soup (I like cream of mushroom) with the wine and then pour the mixture over and around the roast. Sprinkle the seasonings on top of the roast, cover, and place in a 325°F oven for one and one-half hours. Transfer the meat to a hot platter, slice, and pour the sauce over the top. Serves four.

Hungarian Pot Roast

1 3-pound shoulder or neck roast
1 large clove garlic
salt and pepper
1 onion, chopped
2 carrots, sliced thick
½ teaspoon oregano
½ teaspoon parsley flakes
1 stalk celery, chopped
1 cup beef broth or bouillon
1 teaspoon Hungarian paprika
½ cup sour cream

Slice the garlic clove into thin slivers, then insert them into thin knife slits made into the roast. Rub the roast with salt and pepper, then brown the roast in a skillet using a bit of oil. Place the roast in a pot and add all the remaining ingredients except the sour cream. Cover the pot and with the stove burner on low heat slowly simmer the roast for one and one-half hours or until it is tender. Transfer the roast to a hot platter and slice, then ladle the vegetables over the meat, using a slotted spoon. Add the sour cream to the broth in the pot, turn the heat up, and cook until the sauce is steaming, then pour over the sliced pot roast. Serves four to six.

All-in-One Pot Roast

1 2-pound shoulder or neck roast
salt and pepper
4 potatoes, cut into large chunks
4 carrots, cut into large chunks
1 can green beans, drained
flour or corn starch, as needed

In a skillet or deep pan, sear the roast on all sides until it is brown, then transfer to a pot. Pour hot water into the pot until it comes up halfway on the side of the roast. Sprinkle with salt and pepper, cover the pot with a lid and begin slow cooking with the stove burner heat turned on low. After forty-five minutes of simmering, place the potato chunks in the pot. After another thirty minutes, add the carrots and green beans. Continue to simmer until the vegetables are tender. Transfer the meat to a hot platter and slice. Use a slotted spoon to transfer the vegetables to a hot dish. Then thicken the gravy with just a bit of flour or cornstarch and pour over the pot roast slices. Serves four.

Creamed Sirloin Tips

2 pounds sirloin tip steak
meat tenderizer
1 onion, finely chopped
2 tablespoons butter
$\frac{1}{2}$ cup water
2 tablespoons flour
$\frac{1}{2}$ cup sour cream
1 4-ounce can mushrooms

Sprinkle meat tenderizer over the steak meat, then gently pound it into the meat with the sharp edge of a meat hammer. In a skillet, saute the onions in the butter until they are clear. Now use a knife to cut the sirloin tip steaks into triangular-shaped wedges and sear these in the skillet, over medium heat, with the onion until the venison is brown on all sides. Reduce the heat to low, add one-half cup water, cover the pan, and slowly simmer for half an hour. Meanwhile, stir the flour into the sour cream. When the meat is tender, add the cream mixture and mushrooms to the skillet, cover, and allow to slowly bubble for another twenty minutes. The creamed sirloin tips can be served as-is, or ladled over a bed of noodles. Serves four.

In braising venison, the meat is first seared on both sides in a pan. The temperature is then reduced to a slow-bubble, other ingredients are added, and then the pan covered and allowed to simmer on low heat.

Venison Scaloppini

2 pounds round steak
6 tablespoons olive oil
2 teaspoons garlic powder
1 12-ounce can tomatoes
1 teaspoon oregano
1 teaspoon parsley flakes
1 teaspoon salt
½ teaspoon black pepper
4 slices mozzarella cheese

Cut the round steaks into four equal portions. In a skillet, blend the garlic power into the olive oil, then brown the steaks on both sides over medium-high heat. Add the tomatoes and sprinkle the seasonings over the tops of the steaks. Reduce the heat to low, cover the pan, and slowly simmer for forty-five minutes. Spoon the tomatoes and juices into an oven-proof platter, arrange the steaks on top, then lay a slice of mozzarella cheese on top of each of the steaks. Slide the dinner platter into an oven preheated to 400 °F until the cheese is melted and just beginning to brown. Serves four.

Venison Swiss Steak

½ teaspoon salt
¼ teaspoon black pepper
flour
2 pounds round or sirloin tip steak
1 cup cooking oil
1 green pepper, chopped
2 onions, sliced
1 8-ounce can tomatoes with liquid

Blend the salt and pepper with flour, then gently pound the mixture into both sides of your steak with a meat hammer. Now cut the meat into four equal portions. In a skillet containing several tablespoons of oil, brown the meat on both sides. Add the pepper, onion, and tomatoes (with packing juice), cover the pan, reduce the heat to low, and slowly simmer for one hour. Check after one-half hour and add a bit of water to the pan if necessary. Serves four.

Barbecued Round Steak

2 tablespoons butter
2 tablespoons cooking oil
1 onion, chopped
2 stalks celery, chopped
2 pounds round steak
barbeque sauce
1 cup beef broth or bouillon
2 tablespoons brown sugar
4 tablespoons Worcestershire sauce
1 medium can tomato soup

Blend the butter and cooking oil in a skillet and saute the onion and celery, then set aside briefly. In the same skillet, brown the round steak. In a separate saucepan, add all the remaining ingredients and simmer for 15 minutes. Place the browned steak in a deep casserole dish, spoon the sautéed onions and celery over the top, then pour the barbecue sauce over all. Cook, uncovered, for one and one-half hours in a 350°F oven. Serves four.

18

Sumptuous Soups, Stews, and Casseroles

oups and stews with venison as the main ingredient undoubtedly
date back to the first primitive uses of fire and food cooked in clay
vessels. However, it wasn't until the medieval 14th-century reign
of King Henry that "stuwe" acquired its official name to identify
the nature of the feast.

Some cooks proclaim that a stew is nothing more than a thick soup.
Others say soup is nothing more than a thin stew. But there are differences
worth noting. There are also many similarities, and there truly is no such
thing as an original or secret recipe. By simply adding a pinch of thyme, sub-
tracting the celery, splashing the pot with just a hint of sherry, or doing any
number of countless other small things, we could concoct supposedly "new"
recipes until the end of time.

Is a stew really
only a thick
soup, or is a
soup really only
a thin stew?
The debate
goes on, but in
either case
venison is one
of the most
popular main
ingredients.

Casseroles generally are stew-like concoctions baked in the oven, often with a topping of breadcrumbs or biscuits.

Incidentally, casseroles loosely fit into the category of stews, and so they'll also be included in this chapter. By definition, a casserole is a very thick stew with a basis of rice, noodles, or potatoes, but unlike a stew, which is generally prepared in a pot on a stove burner, a casserole is prepared in a glass or earthenware vessel and baked in one's oven.

But let's first get back to soups and stews and the main differences between them. For one, the typical assortment of vegetables comprising a soup are generally diced while those going into stews are generally cubed or chunked. The reason for this is that soups traditionally are made on short notice and designed to be eaten just as quickly. Hence, you want to speedily combine all of the ingredients.

Stews, on the other hand, are long-term love affairs that are best eaten only after hours of slow simmering. Consequently, the use of small, diced vegetables, as in soups, would see the stew transform itself into mush; thick hunks of vegetables hold together longer to give the stew body and integrity.

Hearty stews are terrific one-pot meals. Leftovers re-heat easily and freeze well.

Another difference between soups and stews is that soups typically have a broth color ranging from semi-clear to amber, while stews usually reveal

Virtually any combination of vegetables can be used to create a soup or stew. As a rule, stews cook longer, so vegetables should be cut into chunks; soups are cooked more quickly, so vegetables should be diced.

a rich, dark, gravy-like color. The reason for this is that in preparation of soup the venison chunks are either placed in the soup pot raw to steam-cook, or they are just briefly seared in a bit of cooking oil before going into the pot. But in preparation of stew, the venison chunks are usually first dredged with seasoned flour and then browned in a skillet.

Finally, don't make the mistake of using your most tender cuts of venison in soups or stews. The lengthy cooking period, especially with stews, which is necessary to harmonize the flavors of their various components, will turn already tender cuts of venison into soft, limp meat lacking any substance. Instead, use tougher cuts that will hold together through the duration of the cooking and only later become tender.

Last, there are two other important points. Never allow a soup or stew to come to a rolling boil because this will cause the meat to shrink, the vegetables to wilt, and the spices to commit suicide. What you want is an almost arthritic simmer, which reveals faint wisps of steam as tiny bubbles barely pop on the surface. And never allow soups or stews to cook so long that their liquid content begins to evaporate significantly. If this happens, adding a bit of water, stock or wine is the usual remedy.

Don't use your most tender cuts of venison for soup or stew because they'll fall apart. Use the tougher cuts from the front legs and neck; the slow-cooking process will tenderize them and their coarser texture will hold them together. The first step with nearly all recipes is to dust the meat chunks with flour and then brown them in a skillet.

Stormy Weather Soup

1 pound venison, cubed
3 carrots, diced
4 potatoes, diced
2 onions, diced
2 bell peppers, diced
1 large can tomatoes
3 celery stalks, diced
1 large can V-8 Juice
2 tablespoons Worcestershire sauce
2 teaspoons Tabasco sauce
salt and pepper to taste

In a skillet, brown the venison cubes in a bit of oil, then transfer to a large pot. Cover the meat with cold water, then add the remaining ingredients and slowly simmer for one hour. Serves four.

Stews are traditionally served as complete evening meals while soups are usually served as quick, high-energy lunches accompanied by breads or crackers. But it's not necessary to become a conformist; do as you like.

Venison Minestrone

4 cups dry pinto beans
water
1½ pounds venison, cubed
1 large onion, chopped
6 carrots, chopped
6 stalks celery, chopped
6 tablespoons olive oil
1 large can tomatoes
3 potatoes, cubed
2 teaspoons garlic powder
2 tablespoons basil
½ cup parsley, chopped
½ cup macaroni, cooked
½ head cabbage, chopped
Parmesan cheese

Place the beans in a deep bowl, completely cover with cold water, and allow to soak overnight. Simmer the meat in one quart of cold water until it is tender, then refrigerate overnight. The following day, drain the beans and add them to the pot containing the venison and broth and simmer two hours or until the beans are tender. Meanwhile, in a deep skillet, saute the onion, carrots, and celery in the olive oil. When the vegetables are fully cooked, add the can of tomatoes and simmer until the liquid is almost evaporated, then add this skillet of vegetables to the soup pot along with three quarts of water. Allow the soup to simmer for one hour, then add the potatoes, garlic, basil, and parsley and allow to simmer for one hour longer. Just before serving, stir the macaroni and cabbage into the soup, cover and let sit for at least five minutes. After ladling the soup into bowls, sprinkle about one tablespoon grated Parmesan cheese on top of each. Serves four (with plenty left over that can be frozen for another meal).

Savory Bean Soup

1 pound venison, cubed
1 8-ounce can tomato sauce
1 large can tomatoes
2 tablespoons dried onion flakes
10 cups water
1 medium can red kidney beans
½ teaspoon chili powder
2 teaspoons salt
½ cup uncooked Minute Rice
½ cup shredded American cheese

Add all of the ingredients, except the rice and cheese, to a deep pot and simmer on low heat for one hour. Five minutes before serving, stir in the rice. Ladle the soup into bowls, then sprinkle the cheese on top of each. Serves four generously.

Venison Cider Stew

2 pounds venison, cubed
1 teaspoon dried onion flakes
2 teaspoons salt
¼ teaspoon thyme
¼ teaspoon nutmeg
3 potatoes, cut into chunks
4 carrots, cut into chunks
1 apple, chopped
1 cup apple cider

Brown the venison in a skillet in a bit of oil, sprinkling on the onion, salt, thyme, and nutmeg while stirring continually. Transfer the seasoned meat to a crockpot or stew pot, add the vegetables and apple, then pour the cider over the top. Slow-cook on low heat for at least three hours. If too much of the liquid begins to evaporate, replenish it with a mixture of one-half cup water blended with one-half cup cider. Serves four.

Venison-Mushroom Stew

1½ pounds venison, cut into chunks
seasoned flour
2 tablespoons olive oil
1 teaspoon salt
½ teaspoon black pepper
2 medium onions, quartered
5 potatoes, cubed
3 stalks celery, cut into wide slices
2 green peppers, sliced
2 carrots, cut into wide slices
3 4-ounce cans of mushrooms, liquid discarded
1 can mushroom soup

Toss the venison chunks in seasoned flour and brown in a skillet with olive oil. Place the meat in a crockpot. Add the remaining ingredients, except the mushroom soup. Cover the ingredients with water and cook for three hours. If the water begins to evaporate, add a little more. About thirty minutes before done, add the mushroom soup and stir in thoroughly. Serve over hot white rice or buttered noodles.

–Kate Fiduccia

Winter Day Stew

2 pounds venison, cubed
¼ cup bacon drippings
1 onion, cut into chunks
2 carrots, cut into chunks
2 stalks celery, cut into chunks
1 4-ounce can mushrooms
3 potatoes, cut into chunks
2 medium cans beef or chicken broth
1 cup port wine
2 tablespoons Worcestershire sauce
1 teaspoon brown sugar
½ teaspoon cloves
½ teaspoon cinnamon

In a skillet, brown the venison and onion in the bacon drippings. Transfer the onion and venison to a stew pot, add the remaining ingredients and simmer three hours. If the stew becomes too thick, add more broth or wine. Serves five generously.

Deer-Me Casserole

2 pounds venison, cubed
1 medium can condensed cream of mushroom soup
1 cup canned tomatoes, with juice
1 envelope dry onion soup mix
½ cup seasoned bread crumbs

Arrange the meat cubes in the bottom of a casserole dish, then pour the mushroom soup (undiluted) over the top. Sprinkle the onion soup mix, then pour the tomatoes and juice over the top. Cover the dish and bake at 325°F for two hours. During the final fifteen minutes of cooking, remove the cover from the dish and sprinkle the top of the casserole with the breadcrumbs. Continue baking until the breadcrumbs are nicely browned. Serves four.

Venison Stroganoff

½ cup butter
1 teaspoon garlic powder
1 ½ pounds venison, cubed
1 cup flour
1 onion, chopped
1 tablespoon salt
¼ teaspoon black pepper
1½ cups water
1 cup fresh mushrooms
1¼ cups sour cream

In a skillet, melt the butter and then stir in the garlic powder. Flour the venison chunks and then brown them in the skillet. Add the onion, salt, and pepper, then stir in the water, cover the pan, and simmer slowly for forty-five minutes. Now add the mushrooms and sour cream and continue to cook another fifteen minutes, but do not allow the sauce to come to a boil. Traditionally, stroganoff is served over a bed of thick Pennsylvania Dutch noodles, but for variety you can use thin oriental noodles or rice. Serves four.

West Texas Venison Casserole

2 pounds round steak or sirloin tip steak
1/4 cup flour
1 teaspoon salt
1/2 teaspoon black pepper
1/4 cup bacon drippings
1 stalk celery, chopped
3 onions, sliced
2 tablespoons Worcestershire sauce
2 cups tomatoes, with juice
1 8-ounce package wide noodles

Cut the venison into four or six equal pieces, then dredge in a mixture of the flour, salt, and pepper. Brown the meat on all sides in a high-sided skillet containing the bacon fat. Add the celery and onions and continue cooking over low heat until the onions are clear. Add the other ingredients, except noodles, cover the pan, and cook slowly for one and one-half hours or until the meat is tender. Prepare the noodles according to the package instructions. Then place the noodles on a hot serving platter, carefully lay the venison pieces on top, then pour the sauce from the pan over the top. Serves four.

Cheddar-Noodle Casserole

1 pound venison, cut into cubes
1 stick margarine
1 small onion, minced
1 4-ounce can mushrooms, with liquid
1 teaspoon Worcestershire sauce
1 bay leaf, crumbled
1 8-ounce package noodles
1 cup milk
1 teaspoon salt
1/4 teaspoon black pepper
1/2 cup grated cheddar cheese
1 cup seasoned croutons

In a skillet, brown the venison cubes in two tablespoons of the margarine, then stir in the minced onion and cook over low heat until it is clear. Drain the mushrooms and set aside, pouring the packing juice from the mushroom can into the skillet with the meat and onions. Add the Worcestershire sauce and bay leaf, stir well, cover the pan, and simmer on low

Although casseroles are stew-like concoctions, they're unique in that venison burger is usually used instead of meat chunks, and some type of pasta is added such as rice or noodles.

heat for thirty minutes. Prepare the noodles according to the package instructions, then drain. Stir the remaining margarine into the hot noodles until it is melted, then add the venison cubes, pan juices, milk, salt, and pepper. Transfer to a buttered casserole dish, then sprinkle the cheddar cheese on top. Now sprinkle the croutons on top. Bake at 325°F for one hour. Serves four.

Hunter's Favorite Pie

2 pounds venison, cubed
2 tablespoons butter
2 onions, diced
1 teaspoon garlic powder
1 large can tomatoes
1 tablespoon paprika
$\frac{1}{2}$ teaspoon red cayenne pepper
1 bay leaf, crumbled
$\frac{1}{4}$ teaspoon thyme
1 cup beer
3 carrots, sliced thinly
1 package frozen peas
1 tube biscuits

In a skillet, brown the venison in the butter. Then stir in the onions, garlic powder, tomatoes, seasonings, and beer. Cover the pan and simmer slowly for one hour. Stir in the carrots and peas, cover, and simmer fifteen minutes longer. Transfer the mixture to a deep casserole dish and arrange biscuits on top. Now bake at 400°F for fifteen minutes or until the biscuits are nicely browned. Serves four.

19

What To Do With All That Burger and Sausage

O f all meat products grown in this country, hamburger is the most widely consumed. According to the American Beef Council, every adult consumes an average of thirty-one pounds of hamburger per year in one form or another. Deerburger is equally versatile. And because it's lower in fat and cholesterol than beef, it's more healthy. Use deerburger in any manner in which you'd use hamburger.

Although not as widely used as burger, bulk venison sausage and links also are popular in hunting households. Our favorite uses for them are included in this chapter, as well.

Before offering specific burger recipes, we should point out a few important aspects of using this particular ground meat. First, because of its fat content (which we added at grinding time, usually in the form of suet), it is not necessary to add any cooking oil to a skillet or griddle before frying burgers. It is wise, though, to sprinkle just a bit of salt onto your cooking surface, as this will prevent the meat from sticking and scorching until the fat in the meat has had a chance to render-out slightly for the remainder of the frying.

Second, most grocery stores and meat markets that grind burger use the tougher cuts of beef. Likewise, hunters commonly use scraps, trimmings, and tougher cuts in their burger. But many hunters also commonly use their most tender cuts of venison, throwing into the burger-to-be pile pieces of rump meat and end-cuts from backstraps. This can result in burger that is so tender it may begin to fall apart in the pan. This poses no problem if you're merely browning the meat before adding it to spaghetti sauce, chili, and the like, but it's annoying when you're trying to fry deerburgers.

The solution is to add some type of flavorless binder to the burger just before forming the burger patties with your hands. The best binder combination I've come across is one slice of fresh, crumbled bread, an egg, and a

181

Some hunters have been known to push their entire deer through a meat grinder. But even if you grind only the tougher cuts, scraps, and trimmings, you'll still have upwards of forty pounds of burger and sausage.

bit of cold water for every one pound of burger. Add the burger and binding ingredients to a bowl and knead them together with your hands; then make each individual burger patty in the usual way.

If your family begins to tire of deerburgers prepared in the customary manner, try adding a little flare to your burgers. Before forming them into patties ready for the skillet, add a splash or two of Worcestershire sauce, A-1 steak sauce, or barbecue sauce, kneading it thoroughly into the meat. For still different variations of burgers, knead into the ground meat a bit of

Venison burgers, especially when a fancy recipe such as Burgers Al Fresco is used, produce eventful meals to be proud of.

finely chopped sweet onion and garlic powder, or a combination of sweet basil and thyme. One of the simplest and yet most delectable ways to enjoy your burgers is to sprinkle them with nutmeg while they're frying for a unique nutty flavor.

Other popular uses for all that deerburger you've created include the following:

Venison Burgers Al Fresco

1 pound deerburger
1 egg, slightly beaten
½ cup sharp cheddar cheese, shredded
¼ cup fresh broccoli, finely chopped
1 teaspoon Worcestershire sauce
1 clove garlic, finely chopped
1 tablespoon onion, finely chopped

Mix all ingredients together and make into four patties and fry or grill for five to six minutes per side. Serves four.

–Kate Fiduccia

Venison Meatloaf

1 ½ pounds deerburger
2 slices fresh bread, crumbled
2 eggs
1 8-ounce can tomato sauce
½ cup onion, chopped
1-½ teaspoons salt
1 medium bay leaf, crumbled
dash thyme
dash marjoram

In a bowl, combine all ingredients and knead together with your hands. Dump the works into a bread pan and tap to settle the contents. Bake at 350°F for one hour. Serves four.

Deerburger Chili

2 pounds deerburger
1 green pepper, chopped
2 16-ounce cans red kidney beans, with liquid
2 12-ounce cans whole tomatoes with liquid
1 tablespoon red cayenne pepper
2 tablespoons garlic powder
1 teaspoon ground cumin powder
4 tablespoons chili powder
2 bay leaves, crumbled

Brown the deerburger in a skillet, then spoon off the grease. Add the burger and remaining ingredients to a deep pot along with one quart of cold water. Slowly simmer on low heat for two hours. Serves eight.

Venison Meatballs, Noodles, and Gravy

1 $\frac{1}{2}$ pounds deerburger
3 slices fresh white bread
2 teaspoons salt
$\frac{1}{4}$ teaspoon black pepper
$\frac{1}{8}$ teaspoon basil
$\frac{1}{8}$ teaspoon oregano
$\frac{2}{3}$ cup chopped onion
$\frac{1}{4}$ cup butter
1 10-ounce package wide noodles
1 cup milk
1 tablespoon flour

Crumble the bread and knead it into the deerburger with the salt, pepper, basil, oregano, and onion. Now form one-inch-diameter meatballs with your fingers. Place the meatballs on a cookie sheet and chill in your refrigerator for one hour, then brown the meatballs in a skillet containing the butter, turning them frequently. Reduce the heat under the skillet to low, cover with a lid, and let the meatballs continue to cook slowly for another fifteen minutes. Meanwhile, cook the noodles according to the package instructions, then drain. Transfer the meatballs from the skillet to a plate in your oven to keep them hot. Add to the drippings in the skillet the milk and just a pinch of the flour at a time, constantly stirring on medium-high heat until it turns into a rich gravy. Add the meatballs to the gravy, stir gently, then ladle over the top of the bed of noodles on a hot platter. Serves four generously.

Venison Goulash

1 4-ounce package wide noodles
1 pound deerburger
1 onion, chopped
½ cup ketchup
3 stalks celery, chopped
1 4-ounce can sliced mushrooms
1 14-ounce can tomatoes, with liquid
2 teaspoons salt
½ teaspoon black pepper

Cook the noodles according to the package instructions. Meanwhile, brown the deerburger in a skillet. Drain off the grease, then add the onions and continue cooking until they are clear. Stir in the cooked, drained noodles, ketchup, celery, mushrooms, tomatoes, salt, and pepper. Cover the skillet with a lid and simmer on very low heat for one-half hour. Serves four.

Chicago!

1 pound deerburger
2 teaspoons butter
2 8-ounce cans tomato sauce
½ teaspoon salt
½ teaspoon Worcestershire sauce
1 8-ounce package cream cheese
1 8-ounce carton small-curd cottage cheese
¼ cup sour cream
1 green pepper, chopped
¼ cup scallions, minced
1 6-ounce package wide noodles

In a skillet, melt the butter over medium heat and brown the deerburger, then spoon off grease. Stir in the tomato sauce, salt, and Worcestershire sauce, and allow to simmer on very low heat. In a separate bowl, blend the cream cheese, cottage cheese, and sour cream, then stir in the green pepper and a bit of the scallions. Prepare the noodles according to the package instructions, then drain. Stir the noodles into the cheese blend. Butter the inside of a casserole dish, then spread the noodle-cheese mixture in the bottom. Spoon the meat and tomato sauce on top of the noodles and sprinkle with the remaining scallions. Bake at 350°F for forty-five minutes. Serves four generously.

Grill venison sausages the same way you would those made of beef or pork. They're also terrific when added to casseroles.

Favorite Ways to Cook Sausage

Venison sausage, whether in bulk form, links, or rings, can be cooked and served exactly the same as you would their beef or pork counterparts purchased at your grocery store.

To make sausage sandwiches, form patties from bulk sausage and fry as you would burgers, then serve on sandwich rolls. As a pleasing variation of this, melt two tablespoons of butter in a skillet. Then knead into the equivalent of each intended sausage patty one egg, one teaspoon of water, and one-quarter teaspoon parsley flakes. Form into patties and fry in the usual way. When the sausage patties are almost done, top each with a slice of mild cheddar cheese and cover the pan briefly. When the cheese is melted, serve each sausage patty between two slices of buttered rye toast.

When using sausage links or ring sausage for sandwiches, I like to fry them slowly on low heat and, when they are cooked all the way through, slice them lengthwise and serve in Italian buns with a heap of green pepper strips and onion slices that have been seared in a bit of olive oil.

Link and ring sausage can also be slow-cooked in a skillet, refrigerated, sliced thin, and served as hors d'oeuvres with assorted cheeses and crackers.

Try these favorite recipes:

Sausage Supreme

1 pound bulk sausage
1 onion, chopped
2 teaspoons Worcestershire sauce
1 teaspoon garlic powder
3 carrots, grated
1 8-ounce package "curly" noodles
1 can condensed cream of mushroom soup
½ cup Parmesan cheese

In a skillet, brown the sausage, pour off the grease, then stir in the onion and Worcestershire sauce. When the mixture begins to bubble, stir in the garlic powder, then turn off the heat. Prepare the noodles according to the package instructions, then drain. Now stir the noodles, sausage mix, carrots, and soup together until they are well blended. Pour into a buttered casserole dish and bake in a 350°F oven for twenty minutes. During the final four minutes of cooking, sprinkle the Parmesan cheese over the top. Serves four.

Country Casserole

1 pound bulk sausage
1 onion, chopped
1 green pepper, chopped
1 16-ounce can baked beans
1 8-ounce package elbow macaroni
½ cup tomato juice
½ teaspoon salt
½ cup grated mild cheddar cheese

In a skillet, brown the sausage in a bit of cooking oil, spoon off grease, then stir in the onion and green pepper and continue to cook on low heat until they are tender. Meanwhile, cook the macaroni according to the package instructions, and drain. Blend the macaroni and sausage mix, then transfer to a large casserole dish. Stir in the beans, tomato juice, and salt. Mix thoroughly. Bake in a 400°F oven for twenty minutes until the casserole begins to bubble. Then sprinkle the cheddar cheese on top and bake five minutes longer. Serves four.

Espagnole

8 large sausage links
3 cups white rice, cooked, keep warm
¼ cup chopped onion
¼ cup chopped green pepper
1 12-ounce can tomatoes, drained
1½ teaspoons salt
½ teaspoon black pepper

Fry the sausage links in a skillet containing a bit of oil until they are thoroughly cooked. Remove the sausage links from the pan and slice them into half-inch thick "rounds." Add the onion and green pepper to the drippings in the pan and cook until the onion is clear. Now stir in all the remaining ingredients and cook, uncovered, over low heat for fifteen minutes. Serves four.

Venison Ragout

8 large sausage links
1 cup chopped onion
½ teaspoon garlic powder
1 green pepper, cut into half-inch strips
1 12-ounce can tomatoes, drained
2 tablespoons paprika
¼ teaspoon black pepper
½ teaspoon salt

Gently fry the sausage links until they are thoroughly cooked, then cut them into one-half-inch thick "rounds." In the same pan, saute with the onions and garlic powder until the onions are clear. Add the green pepper, tomatoes, sausage pieces, and seasonings. Cover and simmer over low heat for thirty minutes. Meanwhile, prepare a bed of boiled new potatoes, white or brown rice, or noodles, and transfer to a hot serving platter, then ladle the ragout on top. Serves four.

I hope you will find butchering and preparing your own venison to be a satisfying way to enjoy nature's bounty. May it bring many scrumptuous meals to your family and friends.